Cecil Walsh (1869–1946) was a judge of the High Court in the northwest provinces of India before Independence. His other works include *Indian Village Crimes* and *The Advocate: His Aims and Aspirations*.

THE AGRA DOUBLE MURDER

A Crime of Passion from the Raj

Cecil Walsh
Foreword by Ruskin Bond

SPEAKING TIGER PUBLISHING PVT. LTD
4381/4 Ansari Road, Daryaganj,
New Delhi–110002, India

First published in Great Britain 1929

Published in India by Speaking Tiger in paperback © 2017

ISBN: 978-93-86582-92-8
eISBN: 978-93-86582-91-1

10 9 8 7 6 5 4 3 2 1

The moral right of the author has been asserted.

Typeset in GoudyOlSt BT by Jojy Philip
Printed at Thomson Press India Ltd.

All rights reserved.
No part of this publication may be reproduced,
transmitted, or stored in a retrieval system, in any form or
by any means, electronic, mechanical, photocopying,
recording or otherwise, without the prior
permission of the publisher.

This book is sold subject to the condition that it shall not,
by way of trade or otherwise, be lent, resold, hired out,
or otherwise circulated, without the publisher's
prior consent, in any form of binding or cover
other than that in which it is published.

"The annals of criminal jurisprudence exhibit human nature in a variety of positions, at once the most striking, interesting and affecting. They present tragedies of real life, often heightened in their effect by the grossness of the injustice, and the malignity of the prejudices which accompanied them. At the same time, real culprits, as original characters, stand forward on the canvas of humanity, as prominent objects for our special study."

—Burke

"So the only thing is to poison the soup."
—Mrs Fullam to her lover.
(Before murdering her husband.)

"How God has worked out all things so beautifully and brought us two most devoted and loving sweethearts close together, and given us freely to each other!"
—Mrs Fullam to her lover
(After murdering her husband.)

Contents

Foreword ix
Preface xiii
Chronological Table xv

I	Dramatis Personae	1
II	The Story of the Crime	21
III	The Medical Aspect	111
IV	The Two Trials	144
V	Obiter Dicta	153

Foreword

The way of life that forms the background to this human tragedy vanished long ago. It vanished when almost the entire British and Anglo-Indian population left this country in the years leading up to and following Independence. By 1950, the colonial-style bungalow in the cantonments, civil lines, hill stations, were lying empty and going for a song. But during most of the nineteenth and early twentieth century, many of the larger towns, cantonments and railway centres had considerable populations of Anglo-Indians and domiciled Europeans, and their social life was distinct and very different from the social life of the rest of India.

By and large, it was a dull and monotonous life, enlivened only by visits to the 'hills' during the extreme heat of summer. There were clubs, tea parties, occasional dance parties, school fetes, sometimes the church. For the second or third rungs of society—the clerks, junior officials, teachers, nurses, hotel managers, others living on salaries that were just about sufficient to support a family—life in the small towns of India could be drab and soul-destroying. And sometimes it led to a revolt against convention; adultery, an illicit love affair, a crime of passion.

In Mrs Fullam's case, a crime of passion. In Mr Clark's case, a crime of convenience. Both murdered their respective spouses without any scruple. Mrs Fullam used poison— poisoning her husband over a period of time. Clark helped supply the poison. And, impatient to be rid of his own wife, he had her killed by paid assassins.

In the early twentieth century it was often difficult to detect poison in the human system. Hence its popularity as a murder weapon. Many deaths from poisoning were attributed to accident or suicide. Mrs Fullam would have got away with her crime if she had not kept her lover's letters—together they formed a horrifying record of a murder carefully planned and executed. In their infatuation they showed no mercy to their victims, no concern for the consequences or the effect on their children.

When I first read this book some sixty years ago, it left a deep impression on me. Those were the sort of ordinary, next-door folk I had seen and known as a boy. Perfectly harmless and civilized to all appearances. And yet, capable of taking each other's lives out of purely selfish and self-indulgent motives. I found myself alluding to the case in my own stories—in 'He Said It with Arsenic' and, more recently, in Miss Ripley-Bean's recollection of the case in my collection of stories *Death under the Deodars*.

I am told that most murders are committed out of hate or jealousy or simply for profit or property. In this case it was none of those things. A life of sheer boredom led to a passionate entanglement, and this in turn could be furthered only with the help of a little arsenic in the morning tea—on a regular basis!

On a second reading recently, I found Sir Cecil Walsh's resume of events as gripping as when I first read his account of the Agra Double Murder. Although at times his observations reflect the racial prejudices of the period, his presentation of events and his insights into the psychology of the perpetrators and their victims, is quite masterly. No fictional thriller can match this account of a sordid yet haunting crime of thwarted passion.

Ruskin Bond
Landour, Mussoorie

Preface

The planning of this exceptional record of passion and crime caused me some difficulty. It will, perhaps, assist the reader if I explain the plan which I have adopted. I have not printed the evidence as given at the two trials in the High Court, but have allowed for the most part, Mrs Fullam's letters to tell their own tale. So much of the case depended upon her voluminous correspondence, and upon the admissions contained in them, that the oral evidence tendered at the trials covered only a small portion of the ground, other than the medical question, which is dealt with in a special chapter. Much of the testimony called before the committing Magistrate was omitted at the trials. Moreover, the story, instead of being developed as a connected whole, was split up between the two separate charges. Merely to have printed evidence, as given, would have been inadequate, and confusing. I have, therefore, set out the whole story in a connected narrative, with copious extracts from the correspondence, in the nine sections of Chapter II, after describing in Chapter I the personalities, and the positions in life, of the chief actors.

Chapter III contains an examination of the medical history, and aspect, of the case. It has been mainly written by a friend of mine in the Indian Medical Service, who first suggested to me the public interest of the crime. I had hope that he would have been able to carry out his original intention of collaborating with me in the production of the book, but his professional duties prevented him from devoting enough time to the task. The reader will find that some of his extracts from Mrs Fullam's letters in Chapter III overlap those quoted in the various sections of Chapter II. This was inevitable, the quotations being made, in each case, for a different purpose. The final chapter consists of general observations upon this unparalleled case, and upon the character of the remarkable Mrs Fullam.

The following rough statement of mileage will enable the reader to appreciate the distances which separated the two lovers, and which Clark had to travel by rail on his visits to Mrs Fullam. Delhi lies about 40 miles south of Meerut, and Agra about 140 miles south of Delhi, and 180 from Meerut. Dehra Dun, the terminus for Mussoorie, is slightly under 100 miles from Meerut.

Chronological Table

1909	The acquaintance begins
April–July, 1911	Arsenical poisoning of Fullam at Meerut
28 July 1911	The 'heatstroke' Fullam goes to Hospital
14 August 1911	Fullam leaves Hospital
17 August 1911	The second 'heatstroke' Fullam's second visit to Hospital
8 October 1911	Fullam removed to Agra
10 October 1911	Death of Fullam
11 October 1911	Burial of Fullam
17 November 1912	Murder of Mrs Clark
18 November 1912	Arrest of Clark
19 November 1912	Discovery of the letters

January 1913	Committal to trial
27 February 1913	First trial opens
1 March 1913	Verdict
10 March 1913	Mrs Fullam and Clark sentenced Second Trial
13 March 1913	Verdict and sentence
26 March 1913	Execution of Clark
July 1913	Confinement of Mrs Fullam
29 May 1914	Death of Mrs Fullam

I

Dramatis Personae

The annals of crime contain few stories of passion, intrigue, and murder, temporarily triumphant, but ending in sudden and swift retribution, so sordid and, at the same time, so remarkable and engrossing as the Agra Double Murder, which took place in India during the years 1911 and 1912. About the middle of the year 1909 Lieutenant Clark and his wife, who belonged to the India Subordinate Medical service, while stationed at Meerut, made the acquaintance of Mr and Mrs Fullam, of the Military Accounts Department. A strong attachment grew up between Mrs Fullam and Clark. It quickly ripened into criminal intimacy, which was barely concealed from their neighbours, and was well known to some of their friends. Within four years, Mr Fullam had been treacherously poisoned, Mrs Clark had been brutally murdered in her bed, Clark had been hanged, and Mrs Fullam had received a life sentence. A little more than a year later, Mrs Fullam, who had given birth in prison to an illegitimate child, died, and the seven children of these two unhappy marriages had been left orphans.

Lawyers and students of legal procedure will find nothing exceptional, or instructive, in the course of the legal proceedings. The police investigation into the murder of Mrs Clark, which occurred in November 1912, more than a year after the death of Fullam, but which led to the discovery of that crime, and of the whole ghastly plot, was distinguished for shrewd decision and rapid action, working upon scanty clues. It was at once noticed that the thieves who were alleged to have broken into the Clarks' bungalow at the dead of night, and to have murdered Mrs Clark, had not touched Miss Clark who was sleeping in the same room. They had removed little of value, and a bull-terrier, which lived in the house and always barked at strangers, had made no sound. These were peculiar features in a midnight robbery and they aroused suspicion. Enquiries produced contradictory statements from Clark, who was notoriously on bad terms with his wife, and enjoyed an unsavoury reputation. His explanations about his nomadic and mysterious conduct during the midnight hours when the murder was being committed were unsatisfactory, and the English Superintendent of Police took prompt measures by ordering his arrest, and by obtaining a search warrant for the bungalow where Mrs Fullam, the widow, was living under Clark's protection. Then occurred one of the most dramatic incidents ever recorded of a search. Inspector Smith, who conducted it, happened to strike his foot against a tin despatch box, which was underneath Mrs Fullam's bed. There was nothing in this incident in itself, but Mrs Fullam's confusion when she stated that it belonged to Clark was obvious, and significant. The box was removed, and on being examined was found to contain something like four hundred letters, most of them love-letters written by Mrs Fullam, initialled by Clark, and neatly tied up in packets of fifty. The contents of these letters afforded evidence of the plot to murder Mrs Clark. But they did much more. The letters contained damning detail of a long history of overwhelming passion, intrigue, and deceit: and conclusive proof of plans for poisoning Mrs Fullam's husband, and of his cold-blooded murder, a year before. Denials were idle, and the task of the police in reconstructing the double crime, was, thenceforward, simple. The trials consisted of little more than corroboration, and formal evidence linking up the medical testimony and documentary proof, and filling in the detail.

But whatever detective interest and legal instruction is lacking in the story, is fully compensated for by its wealth of psychological interest, and by its exceptional value as a contribution to the study of forensic medicine. It affords an outstanding, if not unparalleled example of a long history of slow poisoning, carried out with a variety of chemical agents, administered by the wife of the victim, who suspected nothing till it was too late, under instructions supplied, together with the poison itself, through the post, by the chief criminal, who was himself a doctor, and the trusted medical attendant of the victim. But this is not all. The exceptional medical aspect of the case is that the compromising letters provide for posterity a contemporaneous, almost daily, record, written with the fidelity usually associated with a private journal, by an anxious, nervous, but enthusiastic pupil, of the effects produced, stage by stage, upon the invalid by the constant administration of the destructive doses.

Nor does the medical aspect of the case constitute its only

absorbing feature. The characters of the four chief figures in the tragedy are disclosed by the evidence with a vividness which is unusual, even in the stories of domestic unhappiness and marital crime, upon which, from time to time, the full light of day is shed in the criminal courts. The simple God-fearing patience with which the unfortunate man, Fullam, bore his long-drawn-out sufferings, the unshaken confidence which he appeared to show to the last in his medical friend who was slowly murdering him, the silent forbearance with which he met his end, asking for God's mercy and for blessings on his children, when he well knew that his death was due to the wife to whom he had been so devoted a husband, sound the depths of human pathos. Not less pathetic are the stoical endurance, and self-sacrifice, of Mrs Clark. For the sake of her home and children, to whom she had devoted twenty years of her life, with all the tender care which distinguishes the nursing profession in which she had been trained, she declined to sever the bonds which bound her to her cruel, lustful husband. She patiently endured to the end, while he abused her, ill-treated and struck her, and reviled her to his companions. He consistently neglected her for any other woman who took his fancy, and to her knowledge, made futile efforts to induce her servants to poison her food. Of Clark, it need only be said at this stage that the one redeeming feature of his callous, self-indulgent and repulsive nature, was the fidelity he showed to the mistress whose life he had ruined, accepting with a complacent courage, worthy of a better cause, the well-merited penalty of his amours and blood-lust. With his personality and with the sometimes winning, sometimes horrifying, but always baffling character of Mrs

Fullam, it will be necessary to deal more fully. It is impossible to sum her up in a few words.

All four chief actors were in some way contacted with Calcutta, and belonged, directly or indirectly, to what is known as the Indian Subordinate Medical Department. This body is recruited entirely in India; partly from amongst domiciled Englishmen, but mainly from amongst the Eurasians, or Anglo-Indians, as they are now known. In order fully to appreciate the sequence of events, it is important that the reader should understand, in the first place, the position in life which these people occupied, and in the second place, the characteristics of the society in which they moved. Readers who have lived long in India will find this part of the story easier to follow than those who have only a superficial acquaintance with the domiciled community.

Henry Lovell William Clark, who was forty-two, or a year younger than Fullam, when the story opens, came of a pronounced Eurasian stock. He claimed to belong to an old family, and was proud of it, though he must be acknowledged to have been a reversion to the coarser types from which it had developed. Mrs Fullam in one of her letters refers with obvious satisfaction to her "pedigree gentleman" ("a real pedigree," she emphasizes) and she was disturbed on one occasion by the loss of his "gold family crest" which was evidently a signet which he carried on his watch-chain. She advised him either to have the link made firm, or to lock the signet up. After his condemnation he expressly desired that his sword should be handed over to a member of his family, and this was done.

He was a tall, broad, strongly-built man, with a yellowish rather than brown complexion. His hair was mouse-coloured, rather than black. He had a bullet-shaped head, a low forehead, and a short thick neck. His eyes were fleshy, or what is often called "bloated", but small, and he had a "shifty" expression, betokening cunning and meanness. His mouth, partially concealed under a dark moustache, was large and sensuous, and his general physiognomy was both sensual and of that kind usually alleged to be associated with criminal tendencies. He was a man of poor intellectual calibre. As his daughter once reminded him, with a brutality which sounds hereditary, in a caustic letter which she wrote to him in defence of her mother, he had had difficulty in passing his examinations, and though Mrs Clark could have done better for herself, she waited for him, though not the fourteen years which Rachel had to wait for Jacob, on account of his importunity, while he was trying to qualify. The heavy stupidity and sensuality of his features were reflected in his life and character. But though he was dull and stupid in the sense which counts most in life, and was unable to write a decent letter of average length, or even his love-letters, without assistance, he was clever and cunning enough when he wanted to get the better of anyone. He had the reputation of being a good performer at draughts, and a successful card-player. But though also he played tennis, he had few real friends, unless boon companions in the pursuits of cock-fighting, duck-fighting (a strange sport in which he indulged), and loafing in the bazaar, may be included in that category. He had been rather the "butt" of his fellow-students, and his knowledge of his professional work was slight. There were unfavourable reports about his work, which caused Mrs Fullam anxiety on his behalf, and he seems to have narrowly missed being passed over for his Honorary Commission. He must have lived in a state of hectic excitement, and in an atmosphere of impending catastrophe. This probably explains his phlegmatic attitude after his condemnation to death. He studied the use of poisons with persistency, rather than with any real power of research, but his interest in them was neither academic nor professional, and his power of retention was so small that he was compelled to underline passages which he studied for his murderous adventures, in order to save himself the trouble of hunting them up again for reference. He carried this practice to the length of treating borrowed books in this way, without for a moment considering the use that might be made of it against himself, or the resentment which the owner might feel. He was believed to practice abortion. He certainly obliged Mrs Fullam with drugs from time to time for this purpose, and one may believe that he enjoyed a certain reputation for efficiency because, although dirty both in his appearance and habits, he was, for a man of his small attainments, successful with women. They had other attractions for him as well as being potential patients. He could not leave them alone, and was always engaged in at least two contemporaneous love affairs. Upon the question whether the lady was married or single, he was impartial. He has been described by an acquaintance as "a man of quite repulsive character, with almost repulsive appearance." It must be a continual problem to anyone who studies this story with close attention, as it had always been to those who had met them in Meerut and in Agra, how he managed to capture Mrs Fullam's affections, and to maintain the sway over her which he did. It is one of the mysteries of this tragedy.

Mrs Clark was six years older than her husband and therefore forty-eight in 1910, and was in every way his superior. She was a nurse at the Medical College at Calcutta when she met him. She came of a good, though humble, Anglo-Indian family. She was a quiet, good woman, who devoted herself to her children and her home. She was well aware of her husband's vices and evil-living. She did her best to humour him, but she was a gentle soul, with very little strength of character, and with no influence over him. In the end she came to regard him almost with an air of detachment, but, womanlike, she found excuses, even for him, and complained that his bad companions in Agra had led him astray. She thought they got the better of him, and used him for their own purposes, but she must have persuaded herself of this against overwhelming evidence to the contrary. Her's was the lot of many a domesticated woman in every walk of life, but few of her fellow-sufferers can have left behind them a document so poignant with grief, and so pathetic, as her written review of her domestic life, which is dealt with in Section 8 of Chapter II. It was found amongst her possessions, and admitted in evidence at the trial. From what we know of the children, who gave evidence at the trial, the sons inherited something of her gentleness and reserve, while the daughter possessed not a little of her father's *brusquerie*. Mrs Clark was aware of her husband's attempts on her life, and she showed feminine finesse in countering them, but she had no means except separation of preventing the violent end to which she was foredoomed, and of which she had a sort of presentiment. There was much of the fatalism of the East, and of the phlegmatic Eurasian mentality, about her.

She was probably genuinely jealous of Mrs Fullam; not of her superior attainments, and personal attractions, so much as of the superior appeal she made to her erring husband. It was betrayed by her daughter, and the mother and daughter had no doubt often discussed "the wonderful Mrs Fullam", as Maud Clark sarcastically writes of her to her father. Miss Clark's masterpiece, however, was in the box when the guilty pair were in the dock, and "the wonderful Mrs Fullam" stood before her. She was asked whether her mother had been jealous of Mrs Fullam. "No," she replied, and one can hear the tone in which she sent her shaft across the court, "she was not jealous; she had nothing to be jealous of."

Clark and his wife appear at one time to have lived happily, but he must always have been a great trial to her. He was a headstrong man, with a violent temper, and coarse both in his conduct and language. Four children were born to them at intervals of about two years, but one died in Calcutta. The three who lived, Harry, Walter, and Maud, gave evidence before the Magistrate. They all spoke of the quarrels which had taken place between their parents for many years, and which had become steadily worse as time went on. The elder son spoke of his father having struck his mother at various times since he could remember. It was suggested to him at the trial that there had been some incident, ten years before, at Dinapur, between Mrs Clark and an engine-driver, but Clark had never complained about it, and there is not the slightest ground for supposing that there was any truth in the suggestion. On the other hand, Clark's relations with other women were a constant source of anxiety to his wife, and as he got older they became more open and shameless. The abuse and violent language were all on his side. His favourite expression was to call his wife "a d———d swine," but he was not particular, and his choice of vulgar and abusive terms ranged over a wide field. Maud, in her evidence, told the court that her mother never began the abuse, and that when her father called her names, her mother merely replied, "You are that yourself." Both the sons, as well as the daughter, sided with the mother, of whom they were very fond, and they gradually became alienated from their father, who took very little notice of his family except to supply them with necessary funds. The eldest son said at the trial that his father did not care for his family at all. "He had no love for my mother, and I doubt if he had any love for his children."

At the time when the story opens, Mr Edward Fullam, who was in his forty-fourth year, was Deputy Examiner in the Military Accounts Department at Meerut. He also had worked in Calcutta, where he had met his wife and married her in 1894. She was then only nineteen, or eight years his junior. He was almost pure English, but he must have been domiciled in India, for his father had been a First Class Assistant Surgeon in the I.S.M.D. to which Clark belonged. His mother, who was a widow, lived in Calcutta. He had been to England on leave, and the photograph of him which was produced at the trial was taken there. Mrs Fullam had also been photographed in England. He was the "burra sahib", or head official, of his office in Meerut. His pay was 550 rupees per month, or about £440 per annum, being nearly double that of Clark, and Mrs Fullam appears to have had some money of her own, so that they were comfortably off. He was a quiet, religious man, devoted both to his work, and to his home and children. He was much respected by his acquaintances. He belonged to the Church of England, and taught in the Sunday School. He was a keen volunteer, being a Lieutenant in the local force, and he was also a keen Mason. He was proud of his wife, but tolerated, rather than shared, her indulgence in social festivities.

Augusta Fairfield Fullam was English, though born in Calcutta, and brought up in India. She was thirty-five years old when the story starts. She was the daughter of a Branch Pilot in Calcutta. She had received an excellent education. She read a good deal, being fond of poetry, and of the "trashy" type of novel. She was musical, and both played and sang. She wrote an excellent hand, as may be seen from the facsimile letter in this book. She had a fluent style, could write a newsy letter, and possessed an excellent fund of humour. She and her sisters were reputed, when they lived in Calcutta, to be fond of gaiety, and of bright society. But after her marriage she settled down to a steady domestic life, being an excellent mother, and a good manager. She was distinctly popular, and mixed in society a good deal more than her husband, who was far from strong. He had had a cerebral attack when in England, five years before the story begins, and he suffered a good deal from the heat of the Plains. The type of gossip retailed by Mrs Fullam in her letters to Clark are a clear indication of the sort of society in which they moved, but the Clarks had many acquaintances, especially in Agra, who seem to have been rather a "mixed lot", and who did not belong to the same circle as the Fullams.

Although Mrs Fullam's imperfect features, broad nose, and large mouth, prevented her from being a really pretty woman, she possessed a fascinating personality. She was short, and inclined to *embonpoint*. She had a mass of brown hair, blue eyes, and a bright, pretty complexion. In one of her letters to Clark she writes: "Won't I have a jolly fine time this evening, dancing and looking as sweet as I can in pale blue, which suits my fair complexion so admirably. My dear mother always used to warn me not to be so boastful and vain about my skin and colour, but just to accept it as a blessing from One above." It had become her curse!

She was fond of her children. She describes her motherly pleasure as she carries her little pink and white baby in her arms when she goes to the Post Office for her lover's letter. She often speaks of her anxiety about "Katty," who flagged in the hot season at Meerut, and had to be sent to the Hills. Although she writes to Clark: "You are in love with me, and my Hubby never has been," she had great respect for her husband, not unmixed with a wholesome fear, and when he leaves home for a short visit to the Hills, after one of his attacks, she says that she missed him much more than she would have believed possible. She constantly betrays anxiety lest she should arouse his jealousy, and when he put his foot down on hearing, on his return from the Hills, of Clark's visits to the house during his absence, she makes up her mind that the intrigue must come to an end. She was naturally vain. "I want to be always first in your mind," she writes, "as a pattern of what is good, true and pure," though such a wish expressed to a man like Clark was casting pearls before swine. "I wonder," she says, "if there lives a person in this world who understands my nature. I need all; love, attention and care. I simply cannot share with others. Just a loving, hysterical, weak little creature; but a regular handful. My Hubby says I am a wayward, wilful, headstrong girl." "Surely," she writes on a later occasion, when her husband's death seems imminent, "you would not offer me any position less than that of your wife," (though at that time Mrs Clark was alive and in good health). "You know me well, my darling, and how proud I am." Yet all the time she tried to hold on to her religious principles, as will be seen from time to time in the course of her prolific, and absorbing correspondence. This aspect of her thought and feeling is one of the problems of the remarkable story of her fall. It is not without its pathetic side, particularly as, if she had only realized it, she had almost all that she could want in her husband and children, even though the former was not worldly enough for her.

She possessed great sense of fun, and occasionally wrote quite humorously. On one occasion she relates how they had received an invitation to a "Quadrille Dance". "It is given by the Medical Athletic Club, my darling," she writes, "but what I want to know is who are the athletes? Not Gomes or Theodore, surely! As Portia says: 'God made them so they pass for men.'" Mrs Clark was incapable of anything like this. On another occasion Mrs Fullam quotes from a sentimental song about "Friendship" and adds, "This is part of a dear old song I used to sing when I was a young lady," (a typical error of her class!) "before the bloom was off the peach." When she dreams of the possibility of her lover marrying her, she lets her fancy have full play. Clark had recently received his Commission, and she writes to him, "I hope my Lord Lieutenant Henry William Lovell Clark will lead his second wife up to the hymeneal altar under arched swords of his brother officers, darling." A strange picture to be penned by a married woman, with a young family and a respectable, happy home, to a man who was himself wedded to a wife whom he could only get rid of by murder. It seems incredible, while she was watching and reporting, with every sign of impatience and disappointment, the slow working of the deadly poison which she was administering, that she should have shown, by the most fervent language, a real faith in the power of her God to aid her in reaching what she believed to be her goal of happiness in life. And yet on one occasion, in writing to her lover, she asks him for her sake, not to fail in attending the Baptist Chapel, at least on Sunday evenings. One would like to know the sentiments which Clark expressed to his clerk and confidant, Mr Alick Joseph, when he discussed this subject with him.

It is indeed remarkable how this mature woman, who was not without taste, could have found anything in Clark to attract her. He does not seem to have possessed a spark of humour, nor the least refinement. From the little that we know of them, his letters were terrible compositions, and for the middle newsy parts of many of them he had to fall back upon the egregious Mr Alick Joseph, "the good letter-writer." He ended some of his love compositions with the hope that his "Gussie" was well "as it leaves me at present," which must have grated horribly on her ears. He no doubt possessed virility and physical attractions, and a certain charm for the other sex. Probably Mrs Fullam belonged to that type of woman who likes to be taken by storm. This view is borne out by the first letter from which an extract is given in the next chapter written to Clark in Delhi on the 30th of November, 1910.

Whatever the attraction may have been Mrs Fullam fell hopelessly and incurably in love with the man. The dull respectability of her home may have contributed to it. The liaison was so marked that it became the subject of gossip in Meerut, and was the source of anxiety to the long-suffering Mrs Clark. She even consulted her eldest boy as to whether she should cut the acquaintance with "the wonderful Mrs Fullam", and he advised her to do so. She spoke to her husband about it, but he merely replied with his usual brutishness that he should do as he liked, which, of course, was what she knew he always had done.

The Fullams had been married about fifteen years when the Clarks came to Meerut. They then had three children. Leonard, the eldest, went to school at Kalka. Kathleen, the next, figures prominently in the story. She was very fond of her mother, but was one of the chief witnesses against her in both cases. She was a particularly intelligent child for her age. Frank was a mere infant, and Myrtle, the baby, was born in 1910. Clark attended Mrs Fullam in her confinement, and Fullam believed that both his wife and child owed their lives to Clark. The Fullams lived in quite a comfortable, fair-sized bungalow.

There are certain aspects of the story which may seem strange to readers who are not acquainted with the mode of life in India of the class to which the Fullams and the Clarks belonged. People in a big Station in the Mofussil (country) district are divided into several small social circles, or "cliques". It came out, when the case of the murder of Mrs Clark was investigated, that the friends of the Fullams in Meerut had always entertained suspicions about the cause of Mr Fullam's death. But no breath of suspicion reached the police, or what one may call the upper grades of official, or medical society. Little Kathleen Fullam, wise beyond her years, like many children brought up in India, where precocity is by no means rare, had been warned by her mother to say nothing about her father's death, because by doing so she would cause trouble to those whom she loved. Though she loved her father, who used to romp with his children, and though she was disturbed in her childish way by the indifference which, with that quick and unerring power of observation invariably found in intelligent children, she had noted in her mother during the father's illness, and at the time of his death, she was obedient, and held her tongue for more than a year. If any kind friend had happened to engage her in conversation for five minutes, strong suspicion would have been instantly aroused by what she could have been easily induced to say. But the sudden move from Meerut to Agra just before Mr Fullam's death largely minimized the risk of such a contingency. If the tragedy had occurred in England it is almost inconceivable that it would have been allowed to drop so completely. But in the society in which the Fullams and Clarks lived there is a strange absence of that moral pressure, which, for the want of a better name, is called "public opinion", and which makes the commission of such a crime as the poisoning of Fullam almost impossible without detection. Yet there is no lack of publicity of a certain sort in India. On the one hand, life in bungalows is more exposed to the eyes of neighbours, and to outside observation, than domestic life in England. The number of servants employed in every household, and the constant changes which take place, especially in the lower ranks of society, and in official circles where there are many transfers, and also the way which Indian servants have of talking about the home life of the "sahibs", amongst whom they work, combine to create a constant flow of gossip. Much of it is vague and unreliable. Much of it is deliberately false, and it so often deals with questions of the relations of the sexes, the comparative freedom and independence of women in English society being foreign to Indian ideas and traditions, and little understood, that ugly rumours and slanderous gossip are often discounted, if not wholly discredited, when they reach the ears of Europeans. Within the ambit of their own small circle the members of each are quizzical enough about the conduct of their neighbours. There is much jealousy, and much disposition to criticize. There is, therefore, on the other hand, much circumspection and secrecy on the part of those who fall into temptation and commit breaches of the social law. Nowhere is the great social sin of "being found out" regarded as so unpardonable as in these small circles of large mixed stations in India. This is particularly so in official circles where the great dread is that of discovery by superior officers, which is likely to be followed by official intervention. One result is that the moral tone is not so high, and moral sanctions are not so definitely felt and expressed, as in circles where a healthier public opinion prevails. To such small circles the witty saying of Rochefaucauld that "Virtue would not walk so far if Vanity did not bear her company," may be applied with perhaps greater force than to any other.

It may be said, without offence, that there is to be found amongst some of this class a deficiency of moral courage in their dealings with the ordinary affairs of life, and a consequent inconsistency between their sentiments and their conduct, with the lack of a due sense of proportion. They seem to have a tendency to drift. A surprising example of this failing, so difficult to estimate and so likely to produce unexpected results, is the remarkable mentality disclosed in one of the letters written by Clark to his wife in April 1911, just after he had been transferred from Delhi to the Station Hospital in Agra. He is annoyed because she has neglected to send him his leather case of hair brushes, which had been given to him at Meerut by Mrs Fullam. He writes:

> If you cannot read and understand English please let me know, for then I can write to you either in Hindu or Bengali, as the case may be...If you will take my advice you will either remain in Delhi, or proceed to Meerut, but please do not come here, for the day you place your foot in Agra, you may be quite sure I will promptly resign the service, as I am fed up with your low, disgusting ways, for I am quite sure you don't care a damn what becomes of me, so long as you draw Rs 200 a month. You can go wherever you like, but don't attempt to come near me, otherwise you will know the consequences immediately.

And he closes this torrent of abuse with the following astounding anti-climax:

> Trusting this will find you all quite well, as it leaves me the same, with fond love and kisses to self, and the rest at home.
> I remain, Your affectionate Husband,
>
> H.L. Clark

Another example is afforded by the unintelligible course pursued by Mr Joseph, who seems to have been either an

Anglo-Indian, or an Indian Christian, and a professed friend of the Clarks, when he learned that Mrs Clark was in danger of being poisoned by her husband. He was a young man of twenty-one years of age, who had been at school with the young Clarks, and had recently obtained employment as a clerk at the King Edward Hospital, Indore. He had come from Delhi to Agra in March 1911, with Clark, and had lived for a time with the Clarks. Clark had actually had the grossness to show Joseph Mrs Fullam's letters, and Joseph had written some of Clark's replies, because, as he said, he "was considered in Agra a good letter writer", a poor compliment to Agra's literary resources. Clark had also discussed with Joseph his anxiety to take his wife's life with arsenic, and had even complained that his wife was "poison proof". It is no doubt easier, by the way, for a wife to poison her husband, than vice versa! Before he left for Indore in May, Joseph made up his mind to warn Mrs Clark to be careful about her food and drink! With strange mentality, and in pursuit of the same Christian errand, he took Clark to a Roman Catholic priest to try and secure his conversion. But this was all he did! He failed to warn Mrs Clark. He wrote her a silly letter:

> As I am leaving the station, I wish to have an interview with you. The couplet, "Life is short," recalls to my mind, and as such, no matter what comes in light, I am compelled. Perhaps it is Providential instinct, yet it is a spontaneous wish. Further I wish to tell you something confidential. Trusting you will be kind enough, with all my seeming fault, to give me a personal interview.

To the Magistrate he said, "I got a personal interview with Mrs Clark. I had not enough courage to tell her when I came forward, as I had no proof. So I did not tell her anything. I just talked generally as I was going away." What a miserable confession of imbecility! What wonder that Miss Clark, a young woman of nineteen, with a caustic though hardly engaging style, wrote to her father:

> Please tell Alick Joseph that we don't want his dirty smelling wishes or remembrances. Tell him please to keep them in his dirty pockets as we don't want them.

Clark would no doubt appreciate his young daughter's epistolary style. But Joseph's lack of moral courage did not really matter. Mrs Clark had been well aware for some time that her husband was trying to poison her, and the fact was also known to her children and her servants.

II

The Story of the Crime

1
The Correspondence Opens

Some time in November 1910, Clark was transferred from Meerut Hospital to Delhi. One wonders whether Mrs Clark, or some of her friends had anything to do with it. Such things are done with some frequency and with little difficulty in India. But it was a case, to quote the hackneyed phrase, of "absence makes the heart grow fonder!" and we now enter upon one of the most enlightening, and passionate, series of love letters ever exposed to the public gaze. All of them come from the woman's side. She wrote almost daily, except on Saturdays and Sundays, when her husband was at home. Clark replied with the same regularity, but she dared not keep his letters. Judging from the few specimens in existence, they were not worth keeping, except for the terms of affection, no less ardent than hers, in which they were couched. Indeed, she remarks on one occasion that he frequently copies her expressions.

Mrs Fullam's first letter to Clark refers to the forthcoming visit which he was in the habit of paying to her at Meerut, at least once a month, while he was at Delhi. She expresses surprise that he should want to hear from her as he is to see her so soon, but she does not wish to disappoint him. It is dated the 30th of November, 1910, and ends with the injunction, "Tear up". The envelope was found endorsed "Answered H.L.C. 2/12/10". It begins:

Dear Heart of Mine,

I greet you with loving thoughts and true, and pray that every happiness may be vouchsafed to you.

I am so very glad to know that you will be here in Meerut to-morrow, Harry darling, and once more we shall meet and be happy. Oh! darling, I, too, am counting the hours as they pass, like any schoolgirl. How boyish and youthful you are, my own darling, to act over me just like a young lover over his first love. I know full well that I am not your first love, Harry darling, but I also know and believe that I am the first one you have ever truly fallen in love with. Very late in life has true love met you, darling, and to think that poor I have won your heart, and hold you spellbound. Why can't you give me up for "Mabelle"? (Their fancy name for Mrs Clark). She came first in your affections, my sweetheart. You just wait till I see you to-morrow, darling, and see if I don't talk you into sound common sense, and proper reasoning. But really in your presence I seem to melt and become like wax, instead of being strong and making you listen to me. You are just like Harry Middlemore. Do you remember the book?

Fondest and truest love and kisses, darling. Warmest love and the sweetest of kisses from your own little loving and ever devoted little sweetheart and Bucha.

Gussie

This was the accustomed ending. Later on it became "Gussie, till death". Each called the other "Bucha". It is Hindustani for "baby", though neither of them had learned the correct Roman Urdu rendering. On the 13th of January, 1911, she wrote:

> You must not say, as you do in your letter, that you come after my hubby, and that he is my first love. My precious darling, you come first before anyone else, but of course, as a wife, I must do my duty, and will do it to the end. What say you, Harry, darling?
>
> Last evening's Christmas Tree was quite a success, and Eddie (Mr Fullam) made a fine old Father Christmas. He borrowed a white wig and beard from Mr Myers, and a long red cloak from Mr Symonds of the Hotel. So many little ones were made happy, and every one liked and admired our purchases from Delhi.

On the 3rd of February she tells him that she has been fretting herself ill over what he has called their "petty lovers' quarrels," which she says are very real indeed to her. She also tries to console him on the subject of an unfavourable report which has been made officially about him. He fears it may jeopardize his chances of getting the Commission to which he has been looking forward. The fact was that the Medical Officer was dissatisfied with his frequent absences on leave to go to Meerut, and it was this which soon afterwards led to his transfer to Agra. She writes:

> Oh, sweetheart, dearest, I wish I were near you now in the time of your despondency, to put my loving arms round your dear neck, and kiss all your troubles and fears away. But although I cannot do this as I wish, take heart my own love,

> for my sake, and keep doing your duty, both at home to wife and family, and also at work with cross-grained officers.
>
> Sweetheart, I told you yesterday that Myrtle (the baby) and Mick (the dog) are great chums. She plays with him and he is so gentle and nice with her. We have had Myrtle photographed twice, but no good results. I am so cross over it.

There are indications in the letters that they believed that Myrtle was really his child, and Mrs Fullam's fears about her own condition in the middle of February are the first revelation we find of that curious mingling of deliberate misconduct and criminality with apparently sincere expressions of deep religious fervour, which presents one of the most difficult problems in her remarkable character.

> This time last year I was laid up with Myrtle. Harry, darling, my very own precious sweetie, my worst fears are now realized, and I am quite sure I am caught again. I have been feeling very sick the past two evenings, but last evening suddenly, I got so sick and vomited freely. Eddie had a good laugh, and said, "Now I hope you are fully convinced."
>
> So there is no doubt about the matter now, my Bucha, and we must simply grin and bear it. We have fought and struggled against this, but we cannot fight against God's will, and neither do we wish to. What say you, my own darling? So now you can think when you are playing tennis and enjoying yourself of an evening, how your poor little girl is keeping a rough time, feeling so sick and miserably wretched.
>
> Thy way, not mine, O Lord,
> However dark it be;
> Lead me by Thine own Hand,
> Choose out the path for me.

> I dare not choose my lot,
> I would not if I might;
> Choose Thou for me, my God,
> Then shall I walk aright.
>
> These lines are just what my poor sentiments now express, Harry darling, my very own precious sweetheart, Bucha, and whatever happens, I leave all to God's Almighty will.
>
> Sweetheart darling, I have shown your confidential extract to my hubby, and he thought it a very bad one. He thinks it will be in the way of your getting a commission soon, as one who can only hold a small charge is incompetent to hold a commission, darling. However, he thinks the report is very unfair, in its statement of your knowledge being superficial. Darling, do not you worry over it, everything will come right.

This was written on the 22nd of February, her husband's forty-fourth birthday. The cloud which was hanging over her soon passed away, though not without physical suffering, due to medicine supplied by Clark. Meanwhile, Clark had received his transfer to the Agra Station Hospital. On Wednesday, the 15th of March, he came over to Meerut, and Fullam's suspicions were aroused, as the following letter shows:

> Thursday, 16th March
>
> My Own Dearest Lovie,
>
> I am enclosing the letter which I wrote you yesterday, but had not the chance of giving you, my own darling boy.
>
> Sweetheart, darling, my hubby is very angry with me, it appears he was in the verandah this morning at 5 a.m., and saw you talking to me at my bedroom door. He did not

see anything beyond our whispering together, but that was enough to make him jealous and angry. He was surprised at me in my nightgown, to be saying the last word to you, my darling. We shall have to be awfully careful now, my very own precious Bucha darling. I think perhaps you had better leave for Agra without seeing me anymore, Harry, darling, as it only makes things harder for me, darling love.

Oh, how hard it is for us to struggle against such odds and disadvantages, my own sweetheart, when we love each other so much! God help us. I feel very sorry for you, and pity you, with all my heart, darling, and you know I would gladly help you if I could, but I am helpless and powerless, Bucha darling, and can only ask you to wait for me, till I can come to you free and unfettered, dearest love of mine.

Can you be brave enough to do this, Harry, darling, can I trust you to be a good boy for my sake? God bless and keep you, my own precious treasure.

Nothing, however, could curb the ardour of Clark's courtship. In spite of her warning he was over in Meerut again on the Friday. She writes on Saturday:

My darling, you will be glad to hear that the storm has cleared from our horizon, and things are once more bright and clear, my own sweetheart. Oh! How glad I was to see you on Friday, Bucha darling. I firmly believe in mental telepathy after that, for I seemed to *know* you were coming presently in spite of your letters saying you would not come. Are you comfortable, and have you a nice medical officer, dearie? You are far better away from the dreadful naggings and scoldings you used to get at home, my darling, and yet I know "it is not good for man to be alone."

Here she throws light upon the strange ideas of justice, and the lack of logic, in an infatuated woman. She might at least have realized from her husband's jealousy that Mrs Clark, too, had the right to complain and scold her own husband for his neglect, and his undisguised devotion to another man's wife, which Mrs Fullam fondly hoped could be concealed both from her husband, and from Mrs Clark. At the same time she betrays a touch of vanity in the attention which another man was paying to her, and a subtle suggestion of jealousy over a rumour she has heard of Clark's attentions to another lady.

> I intend to tell you every single thing that happens here in Meerut, so don't get jealous, Harry darling, if I should mention H. having come over. I mean to choke him off, sweetie, as you told me to do, and have no more of his jokes.

In a postscript she adds:

> H. and Eddie have had a most dreadful row. I will write and tell you about it tomorrow. It's nothing about me.

On the other hand, she writes in the same letter:

> Sweetheart, darling, how did you enjoy the dance you had with Mrs S—— the night of the Masonic Dance? You might have told me all about it, Harry dear, and not deceived me. Surely I am not such a dreadful ogre that you are bound to keep things hidden from my knowledge. Does she also write to you, darling? I am not at all angry with you, but I think you might have told me. I would have been better pleased than hearing it from others.

About this time Clark, in an effort to keep pace with his sentimental lady-love, must have burst into poetry. There can be little question that he had received the assistance of Mr Alick Joseph, the "Agra letter-writer". Clark himself was innocent of any literary accomplishments or inclinations. Mrs Fullam writes:

> My sweetheart, your poem is awfully pretty, but your fairy has rather a substantial form, don't you think? Now, my dear old humbug, you won't make me believe that you composed this poem. It's very beautiful and well written. Agra air must have inspired you to great deeds. (She never discovered Joseph!) Just imagine calling me, "A vision sweet of virgin mould."
>
> Oh! Harry, darling, how *can* you? But I can well believe that "Your inmost heart with passions fraught," for I know my darling's nature and temperament only too well. Now to more mundane affairs, darling, as I suppose you are interested to know how fares your girlie. The old story, I am ill and weak. I have made myself ill these last few days worrying and fretting, and for ever having tears in my eyes, darling.

In another letter written about this time, she complains of his want of appreciation of her own ventures into the region of poetry, and indulges in an interlude of gossip about her neighbours, which is characteristic of her outlook on life:

> Yes, darling, the poem I sent you was an original one, I am sorry it was so densely written that you failed to grasp the meaning; however, I won't trouble you to read any more.
>
> Harry, sweetheart, my hubby is not well. There is nothing physically wrong with him, but he is suffering from brain fag, and I fear he will get another attack of cerebral apoplexy like he had five years ago when he went to England. This morning he was telling me he wants to take three months'

leave, and take us all up to the hills. All this worries me so much, Harry, darling, you know I don't wish to go away anywhere, but will let you know how things go, darling sweetheart, mine.

Plague is still very bad here in Meerut, and I suppose the Nauchandi (new moon) will help to spread it. Mrs F. has had another little son, up at Sukkur in the Maternity Home there, so darling, you see your old friend of other days did not join her husband for nothing. You have changed from F. to Fairfield; what an old loving flirt you are my Bucha darling. Now I must not chaff you, for you do not like jokes, I know, but still from your Bucha you can stand anything, can't you, darling? Mrs M., too, has had a son, just the day after her baby completed one year old, and Mr D. of course looks after her.

Oh, Harry darling, my own true, loving sweetheart, you are nothing but an old coaxer to argue with me, and declare you wish to keep up direct communication with me be it as you will, my Bucha darling. I must own that I cannot give you up, your letters are food and drink to me, darling sweet, and I will abide patiently and do whatever you tell me. So let this comfort your tired soul my own pet, and let us await the unfolding of events, my own precious darling.

2
The Plot

The unfolding of events which Mrs Fullam was resigned to await, now begins to take a sensational form. It is at this stage in the story that Clark communicates to her, for the first time, his resolve to use his medical knowledge in order to take her husband's life. He has hinted in one of his letters that they are entering upon a new phase of their existence which will smooth the way for their future happiness. He expresses his intention of coming over from Agra to see her on the 20th of April, and it is at this meeting that he discloses to her his purpose. At the same time she announces to him, while making elaborate plans for giving the visit the appearance of a casual incident, and for avoiding any occasion of jealousy on the part of her husband, that she has made up her mind that their correspondence must cease. None the less, she tempts him by suggesting that there must be some way by which they can finally come together.

"You are a full-blooded man," she writes, "and need a nice, good wife constantly near you, and, moreover, one who will look after you, not nagging and worrying you for ever, but a true help-mate and companion in every sense of the word. Am I not right, my own precious darling sweet?" The alternative of a straightforward confession, with the penalty of mutual divorce proceedings, and the final breaking of the matrimonial bonds which made their own union impossible, never seems to have crossed their minds. Why they should have preferred to embark upon a conspiracy of cold-blooded murder, it is difficult to understand. There may have been insuperable obstacles in the way of a divorce, but what is certain is that a woman who wrote so frankly and volubly about her own feelings and difficulties, must have referred to the subject in the course of this daily correspondence, if it had been mentioned between them, and no trace of the suggestion is to be found. She writes on the 15th of April:

In your every letter lately, darling, you hint that the way will soon be smooth and clear for us. Are you going to decoy me away in a match box? Or, how, Harry, darling? I am beginning to feel quite afraid of you, my big broad-shouldered love, so bold and brave. You remind me, Harry Bucha, of those brave Knight errants of olden days who used to dare and die for their lady love!

Now, darling, let me explain what I want you to say on the 20th. Of course, you must come straight from the station and will just arrive here in time for breakfast. I will be very surprised to see you, and you say that you have obtained a couple of days' leave to take your family back to Agra, I think this excuse will do nicely, Bucha, darling, and you can say you just ran into Meerut to see us all, while your people were getting ready. Then I think you had better ask me for an early dinner, saying you will take the 8 p.m. train back to Delhi, so that my hubby won't be jealous, and when going to Lodge—my darling—do you quite understand?

On the subject of closing the correspondence, she writes on the 19th:

Now I have a statement to make, which I know will upset and worry you, Harry darling, but I cannot help it, Bucha, and it also grieves me more than I can say—but God help us both in this extremity. This is the last letter I can write to you, my heart's own love. There is a crisis impending in both our lives, which I will explain fully on our meeting, darling; but I am not free to do as I please, sweetie. You know I explained this to you before. So I am going to cease all future correspondence, darling, as I shall tell you everything when we meet. Writing is too inadequate to properly express all I have to tell you. Oh, darling, darling, my sweetheart, how can I give you up? I never, never will, but oh, what am I to do? Harry darling, I wish to tell you that on the 20th, when you come, please make the excuse that you have some business to go and see to after breakfast, and that you will be back to tea, so that my hubby will not be jealous. He will be away at the office, and we shall have it all to ourselves when you return, till tea time, lovie, darling. But don't allow him to think that you were closeted here with me all day.

The fateful visit took place, and the two concocted their first plot for the administration by Mrs Fullam to her husband of "tonic" powders, the poison which Clark was to send her. Mrs Fullam stated in her confession, and stoutly maintained to the end, that the plan was to make Fullam so ill that he would be compelled to retire, and to retire to England, while his wife would remain in India. Clark, in an effort to save her at the trial, endeavoured to confirm this. It is probably true, so far as the original inception of the crime was concerned, and it very nearly ended in that way, as the reader will see. But it is quite certain that the ultimate scheme was to kill Fullam outright, and that it received the full assent and co-operation of Mrs Fullam. After Clark's visit to Meerut of the 20th, Mrs Fullam writes on the 21st of April: "We now start afresh with a bright hope before us, shining like a beacon; our star of hope and comfort. So to the winds with trouble and care, darling." She thus describes the success of her efforts to avert her husband's suspicions about the visit:

My precious sweet, how did you get on with your long journey last night, darling? I am longing to hear of your safe arrival, and that all is well with your work. My hubby returned from Lodge, I believe, at midnight, but I was "safe in the arms of Morpheus", so I never knew anything till I asked him this morning. He seems very nice and kind, and never referred, by a single word, to your visit, and neither did I. So you see, darling, in some cases "silence is golden". How much we enjoyed the day only towards the end that wretched K.A. disturbed our peace of mind, and brought a storm of wrath down upon my ears from you, sweetheart darling. Oh, Harry, darling, please don't think any the worse of me for encouraging and laughing so immoderately with that girl and her jokes. If I fall in your estimation, lovie, what good is there in life?

Three days later, she writes her first report of the administration of the powders:

I am sorry I was utterly unable, darling, to send you even a few lines on Saturday and Sunday, as I explained to you, Bucha dearest, that I would have no chance my hubby being at home. You are anxious to know about the "tonic". Well, sweetheart, darling, I have given it regularly since I last saw you.

Contemporaneously with the opening of this phase of criminality, her tortured mind is torn and wracked by pangs of jealousy over her lover's flirtations with a certain Miss W., and she announces her resolve to break with him. This was, probably, only a woman's wile to bind him more closely to her, but it is quite evident that she is genuinely afraid, and suffers acute pangs of jealousy. She describes, in one of her letters about this time, how she went to a dance, after receiving from

Clark a letter which Miss W. had written to him, "her one-time lover and admirer", and which Clark had sent to Mrs Fullam, and how, after putting on a forced air of gaiety, and dancing recklessly, she nearly fainted, and had to be given port-wine, and a warm coat. She adds that when she got home she had a quarrel with her husband which lasted until two o'clock in the morning, and winds up this sad story by expressing her regret that H. is leaving Meerut, because "he would be a kind and useful friend in case I needed one." The trend of this rift within the lute is shown by the following extracts from her letters:

> Do you know, my very own precious Bucha darling, you have made me very jealous by Miss W.'s enclosure. These I consider are incipient beginnings, and it is only an excuse about the cook. She really wishes to make friends with you again, and this is the "thin edge of the wedge". Oh, how silly men-folk are, it's only we women who understand one another's tactics.
>
> Surely in the whole of Calcutta there is a cook to be had? Oh, no, she just wanted an excuse to re-open the old correspondence. Well, Harry, darling, my own precious sweetie, you must now choose between us. Are you an honourable man, or are you not, my darling? Because you cannot correspond with both her and me. If you are going to open up fresh communication, in however friendly a way, Bucha darling, then I cease at once. You know, sweetheart darling, how very jealous and proud your little girlie is, she will have none or all. Anyhow, as I have put my hand to the plough, I will not turn back whatever happens. I can always work, and I may yet live to see Mabelle (Mrs Clark) and self

very happy with your ten children. Oh, sweetheart, darling Harry, my Bucha, my heart is aching to-day. The choice lies with you, and you alone must make it, darling.

~

I read your reply to your old friend, Miss W., which is couched in the most friendly and favourable terms, and I see, darling, with much regret that you are willing, nay, too eager, to do her bidding in every way, and that at once. I am glad you have got her back, Bucha darling. No! I am not glad. It is only my proud spirit makes me write that. Never mind, you decide quick. You are a doctor, and a surgeon, and you must know how the operation hurts, to have one's limb cut off, darling. So my own, my darling love, use the keen sharp knife of separation quickly, and pray do not torture me like this, longer than you can help.

~

Harry, darling, my own precious, dearest Bucha, I am glad to hear you have decided a choice between me and Miss W. But still that does not satisfy me. You must prove to me, darling, that there has ceased all correspondence between you. You say you are surprised at my jealousy, but put yourself in my place, darling, and then think how you would feel if I wrote to a gentleman friend. I know she will surely reply to your letter about the cook, and then if you send him down, she will write and thank you, through mere courtesy, and so on, the beginning will be established! You say, darling, that I cannot blame you, if she chooses to write to you. No, but I do certainly blame you for so eagerly replying and deferring to her every wish—cook, tailing, pillows and all! You could have made heaps of excuses, my Bucha. Lots of work in a large hospital, no time, or better still, need not have replied at all, but darling, I don't want to lecture you on the subject, for you must please yourself. You know my wishes on the subject, you know my jealous disposition, and, sweetie darling, if you love me, as you say you do, then very easily can you prove to me that your love is mine alone.

Oh, this is not imagination on my part, my own darling, as you so lightly pronounce it. How can you say so? Harry, darling, how plausible you are! Just imagine telling me not to worry over trifles, do you call this a trifle, to write loving letters to one girl, and nice friendly ones to another. As for promising on your honour, I am afraid men's honour fails, when a woman tempts. Now I dare say you are very cross and angry with me, darling, but the fault is yours, not mine. However, let this only draw us closer together (if you will).

~

Harry, darling, I have read and destroyed your "copy" of Miss W.'s letter, which you say you have written. Did you only write it, to please me, lovie darling, or have you sent it?

You do not mention that. Never mind, darling, I must accept your word of honour as a gentleman (and a pedigree one at that). But surely she must have replied ere this, considering the cook is wanted sharp. Please let me see the reply, if you don't mind.

My sweetheart darling, I have not yet made up my mind to administer those powders. You have set me a very hard task, Bucha, and I feel afraid, Harry darling. You blame me for compelling you to be rude to Miss W., and treat her in an ungentlemanly way, but what do you ask of your little girlie? Now why do you wish to see me again, dearest? Try not to be impatient, my sweetie; you saw me only ten days ago, and since then you have been quarrelling with me. Miss W. does not really love you as I do—no, never, it is only for her own ends to make use of you, darling. But you are mine, you belong to me by all the sacred lies that exist between us, both past and present, my own darling. Now do not let me start afresh, Bucha darling. You don't realize what a jealous woman suffers.

~

Sweetheart, thanks, thanks for so solemnly vowing and promising to cease all future correspondence with Miss W. You know I could not bear you to take her affection back again. Will you, please, lovie darling, like a good boy, send me her answer to you regarding the cook, &c. Please do not be afraid of any more lectures and jealousies on the subject, but darling, I must know and see how you are going to act.

~

So you have quite forgiven your little girlie and taken me back into your heart again. Oh, Harry darling, I searched minutely every word of your dear letter, and each line, for reference to some tone of regret in giving up Miss W., but I could find none, my very own precious Bucha sweetheart darling. Do you really mean to tell me that you love me altogether far more than she, whom you waited for, so many long years?

~

Sweetheart, darling, my own precious Bucha, let me know if you truly feel any real regret for giving up Miss W., and snubbing her? Am I quite sufficient to atone, all the remainder of our lives, for what you have lost in her darling? Ponder well, and let me have your answer, darling. What would your Buchee do, without her own precious Bucha darling.

~

What a nice long newsy letter this is, Harry darling. I am sure Miss W. never sent you such nice long loving letters, did she? What about her cook, love?

And here this incident, which lasted no longer than about ten days, seems to have closed. The month of April ends with a report that the husband is quite unaffected by the "tonic" powders, and is stronger and better than before, and with some intimate details of marital relations which read strangely from the pen, even of this strange woman, when one realizes all that she was doing:

> My hubby has taken to sleeping out in the back verandah, and Frank's bed is also there at nights, so that his room is empty, and of course I have my own room with Katty and Baby. I told Eddie I feel just like a dried up old maid, or else a widow, without nice loving arms around me; and really I can't sleep for hours every night, darling, just on account of this horrid lonely feeling. My hubby would make a splendid old bachelor or widower, he never wants any love in his life. But I am so different. I can't live without plenty of love and caresses. Eddie says that my second husband will make up for it, so I suppose I must wait for that.

3
April in Agra

The crowded events of the next six months belong to the medical history of the case, which is related in detail in Chapter III, though the stream of Mrs Fullam's correspondence continues its uninterrupted flow, with many domestic details of interest and remarkable revelations of mentality. Meanwhile the Clark household, which consisted of Clark, his wife and daughter, the two sons being at work in Fullam's office at Meerut, passed anything but a peaceful and happy existence in the new surroundings at Agra. Mrs Clark was aware of the correspondence between her husband and Mrs Fullam, but she had not the strength of character, or the will to do more than protest against her husband's treatment of her. If it was not "Gussie", it was some other woman. She had given up all hope of reforming him. When they were at Delhi one of Mrs Fullam's letters was delivered into her hand by the postman. She merely looked at it, and handed it back. She used to talk to her friends in Agra about his behaviour, and one day she remarked that he kept bad company, and "had become very wicked in Agra". She knew that he was making attempts to poison her through the servants.

Clark arrived in Agra alone, to take over his duty at the Station Hospital, leaving his wife and daughter at Delhi. He wrote to his wife the abusive letter which has already been quoted in Chapter I warning her of the consequences of her following him to Agra, and ending with the warmest expressions of affection. The trouble was over the loss of his hair-brushes in a leather case, and the letter was answered by his daughter:

Station Hospital,
Fort Delhi,
8th April, 1911.

My Own Dearest Father,

Thanks very much for your letter, which was not very pleasant to read, but of course we must excuse you, as you must have been told to write like that. But never mind, God will be good to us. He only knows how we four have been treated in the house by you. I am simply shocked at you writing in such a way to mother, over those brushes that wonderful Mrs Fullam gave you. They are not worth two pice to us, and you may rest assured that we all know English, and we are not natives as you imagine us to be. Mother is too quiet for you. You require someone to answer you back in the same way... As for you saying that we worry and annoy you, that's the case with you. Hardly a day passes that you don't row and abuse. If you knew that mother wouldn't look after you, you shouldn't have married her. You proposed to her twice, and then she accepted of you on conditions that you passed your exam. If she only knew that you were going to treat her like a dog in after years, she would have married someone better than you, who would have prized her, and treated her like his queen. As for you imagining that mother does not care a damn for you, I really don't know how you can say that. If she didn't care a button for you or the house, she wouldn't have stood all the kicking and thumping all these years. To my knowledge she is treated very badly, and she has borne it up very patiently.

With fond love and kisses for dearest self.

I am,

Ever your affectionate daughter,

Maud

This is an illuminating document, of a kind seldom addressed by a young woman to the author of her being. She seems to have inherited her father's outspokenness, and one can but admire the girl's loyalty to her mother, and her frank indignation with her father, while one's heart goes out in pity towards the members of this unhappy household.

The family eventually joined their father in Agra. This seems to have happened just after the fateful 20th of April, when Clark visited Meerut and disclosed to Mrs Fullam his plans for trying to poison her husband. Shortly afterwards he made a bold attempt to poison Mrs Clark with arsenic. It is a nice point whether the original efforts were contemporaneous, so that he could study the effects upon his wife in order the better to instruct his mistress how she should dose her husband, or whether the experiment was made on Fullam first. It is certain that an attempt was made on Mrs Clark on 25th April, and the story which came out at the trial is a remarkable one. Clark had had a servant with him during his six months at Delhi whose name was Bibu. He worked both as a cook and as a table servant. He came to Agra with Clark, but he did not like it. There was plague in Agra, and he found difficulty in getting his food in the bazaar. When Mrs Clark arrived he asked for leave, but she would not let him go. He was evidently an honest servant. Soon afterwards Clark called him into his own bedroom, where he slept alone. He told Bibu that he was going to give him a packet containing powder, and that he was to dissolve it in the Memsahib's tea. He would give him another the second day, and another the third day. Bibu asked what it was, and Clark told him not to be afraid, it was only a purgative. He, however, added that he would give him fifty rupees after the third dose, and allow him to go back to his own city, Delhi, but that if he, Bibu, said anything about it he would strangle him. It was to be done with the supper tea. Clark also told him rather tactlessly that the powder was tasteless. The young man had evidently heard of such things, and he "smelt a rat". While the family were having tea that afternoon Clark got up and went out. Bibu then called Mrs Clark into her room, and in the presence of the eldest son, Harry, handed over the packet, unopened. He told his mistress that he had a mother who would die of a broken heart if he were hanged, and that he wished to return to Delhi. This was looking rather far ahead, but he evidently realized that Clark was a determined and desperate man, and that he, Bibu, would certainly be suspected if there was any foul work. Mrs Clark's conduct was ingenious. She asked him not to go. She told him that he might sleep in the verandah so that there would be no risk of the Sahib strangling him in his sleep. But Bibu's mind was made up, and he left for Delhi that night, and never returned. No doubt, when trying to persuade him to stay, Mrs Clark decided that if her husband's idea was to administer poison to her through the cook, it was better to have a cook with a mother and a conscience, who would bring her the poison instead of putting it into her food. She was evidently a woman who thought things out.

The sequel is even more remarkable. Assistant-Surgeon Linton, who was junior to Clark in the same service, happened to be in the Clarks' bungalow that evening, and Harry gave him the powder, and asked him to examine it. This was only an hour afterwards, and Linton took it away with him. He said at the trial that he saw at once that it was a powerful poison, but that he said nothing at the time, except that he would examine it. On examination he found that it was one of the compounds of arsenic. He returned the paper in which the arsenic had been, in a letter evidently written as a blind, without any reference to the powder. When he saw Harry the next evening he told him that it was "a slow poison", but he did not tell him what it was. The inference is irresistible that Linton suspected that Clark had been attempting to poison someone, and that as his inferior in the service, he thought it better to hold his tongue. Anyone who has lived in India will appreciate Linton's conduct and his lack of humanity and public spirit. Linton could hardly have been unaware, even at this time, of the relations between Mr and Mrs Clark. They were well known to everyone in the service, particularly to Joseph, with whom Clark had discussed the properties of arsenic, complaining at the same time that Mrs Clark was "poison proof", and "too quick for him". Joseph had come from Delhi, and was a typical gossip. It is unlikely that he had never repeated any of this to Linton. After this brazen attempt, it was hardly possible for Clark to poison his wife by stealth, and so far as can be discovered, no further attempts were made by him during the year 1911.

4
May in Meerut

Life in Meerut for Mrs Fullam during the hot weather pursued the course which she had marked out for herself, and which she now followed with a strange mixture of confident hopes and guilty fears. Throughout the month of May her daily correspondence with Clark continued in an uninterrupted flow, brimming over with the language of passionate longing, and gushing adoration, mingled with the tittle-tattle of the Station. She lived in a world of romance, and it is difficult at times to know what she really thought, so inconsistent is her voluble vocabulary. Even about the weather she contradicts herself. "My hubby feels the heat terribly," she writes, "and complains of being very tired. But that's an old story, my darling, Meerut is cool and nice, but hot winds and dust prevail all day." The shade temperature in Meerut during the day-time would probably vary between 110° and 115°.

Every day, except on Saturdays and Sundays when she herself is unable to write, she goes to the Post Office to which Clark is addressing his letters and packets of powder to the name of "Mrs Clarkson". She confides to him her domestic concerns, and impresses upon him the importance of economy. She assures him that she is "a very saving person, with an abundance of good, sound common sense." She relates to him a trivial incident of her husband's politeness to a lady friend, which she regarded as a slight upon herself, but seeks consolation in a compliment paid to her by her lady friends, which with the pride of a vain woman she prettily repeats. She and her husband went to an evening party at the G.'s, and a Miss Kitty A., went with them. She tells Clark that:

> It was most amusing to note how careful my hubby was in handing out Miss Kitty from the phaeton! At any other time, I would have become very jealous, Harry darling, but I only thought if my own Harry were here, I should never be allowed to shift for myself. Anyhow, I would rather wait for you, my darling, than let other hands touch mine, even

if they are my hubby's. It was a nice moonlight evening, and
we all sat on the *chabootra*, darling, when suddenly Miss G.
asked me to take off my white silk gloves. I laughed and said,
"I have on no gloves," and then they all remarked that my
hands and arms were so lily-white in the moonlight, they
thought I had gloves. Now darling, I do not mention this for
boasting's sake, no never, but just to show you, my very own
precious love, what a sweet little Buchee darling you have.

The perennial difficulty with children in the Plains during the
hot weather leads to her sending her eldest girl, Kathleen, to
the Hills. The boy, Lawrence, was already away at school in
Kalka. She tells Clark with some pride all about the thrifty
plan which she had made, and asks for his approval:

Katty (Kathleen) is going away to Mussoorie, darling. I am
sending her up with Mrs A., and two daughters, who leave
on Friday, the 12th, my very own precious darling. The child
suffers very much in this heat, and her heart seems weak and
run down. So I am sure the hills will improve her, and then
I will only pay a little towards her keep, darling, and in that,
she will get her tuition and music from the two girls. It's a
good chance, and I am not going to let it slip. What do you
think of this plan, Bucha dearest? I would like to know your
dear opinion because I always like to do what you approve
of. I remember you once said to me the hills would not suit
Katty's heart, but the child seems so run down and upset by
the heat, darling, that I am risking it, and sending her for
a change.

Meanwhile she is working at the task of murdering her
husband by slow poison, and chafing at the slow progress:

> I must say I don't approve of your powders at all darling; how many hundreds of years will they take? Meanwhile, we are constantly running fearful risks, my own darling. However, if it please you, then I am happy.

~

> His complexion has changed to a lovely pink, such as any young lady would envy, darling, and he is full of life and vigour.

~

> Harry, darling, sweetheart mine, and mine alone, those powders are proving themselves a most excellent tonic, and that is about all, darling. My hubby has never looked so well, nor felt so well in all his life, Bucha love. How long am I to continue in this way. I think it would be much nicer to bring about a crisis, soon.

It is not possible to accept the explanation which she afterwards offered in her confession that she was only waiting for her husband's illness, and enforced retirement, and not for his death. The following extracts from other letters in May are a complete refutation:

> We dined outside on the lawn last evening, my Bucha, after returning from the Club. It was so enjoyable and romantic, dining under the moon and on the grass, and it reminded me of your 90 days' leave last year, my very own precious darling, and of how we used to enjoy each other's company at all times, darling. Meerut is so full of you, at every turn, Bucha love. But as you say, darling, brighter days, we hope, are in store for us, which will eclipse past records, sweetie.

~

> I think we will get on A.1 together, dearest love, only I don't know how your grown-up family will tolerate me. I know you will be good and kind to my little ones for my sake, won't you, Bucha?

~

> Oh, Harry, my own precious darling, your letter to-day is one long, yearning cry for your little love. Be good and calm, darling, we will have a nice, long chat on Thursday and talk things over, and see how we can expedite matters that will bring us nearer together, Bucha darling.

The appeals which she makes from time to time to her religion, and her God, and the good influence which she affects to exercise over her lover, have a strange ring about them in the presence of such extracts as these, and the one that follows:

> Sweetheart mine, I missed your letter on Sunday so much. I spent a most wretched and miserable day, and in the evening, although we attended church as usual, I must confess my heart was hot and rebellious, and my thoughts had left Meerut and were far away in Agra wondering what my own sweetheart was doing! Do you remember how I used to tease you on Sundays, by asking if you were going to the city to look for black hens, darling?

(The reference to "black hens" is obvious, certain quarters in every city in India being more or less appropriated to these professional women.)

But all the time she is actually warning him against the possible treachery of his own wife, who would not willingly harm a fellow-creature. It is evident that Mrs Fullam was too wrapped up in herself ever to have tried to understand Mrs Clark, and that she accepted at their full value the accusations which Clark was in the habit of making against his wife's nagging disposition and neglect. "Glad am I," writes Mrs Fullam, about this time, "to hear that you are well again, my own darling, and your throat better. I was feeling anxious and worried, darling, as I know that your wife is not to be trusted, and she may do anything, at any time, to you, Harry darling. Be careful of her, my love." Some of the powders were lost in the post. Anyone who has lived in India can well believe this. But it caused the mercurial Mrs Fullam some alarm, and at her request Clark brought some with him when he visited her on Thursday, the 18th of May. She writes on the 19th:

> It is now just after breakfast, and I sit down to reply to your most loving and lengthy letter, brought to me yourself yesterday, sweetheart. It is so dull here to-day, and I miss you so much, lovie darling. Would that I were always near you, darling, or at least had some hopes of seeing you every day. Oh, what a powerful thing is this love, that has the power to make glad or sad according to circumstances?
>
> How did you reach home, my sweetheart? I hope safe and well. My hubby came home at 12 from Lodge, and I had had a good sleep and just woke, lovie. He asked what time you left, and I said the tonga came for you after dinner, and you went to see your son, which was quite true, was it not, Bucha darling? Did you see your son? My hubby has not referred to your visit, by another word, sweetie, and so I have been perfectly silent too.

> Well, now, did you have a nice, enjoyable day, Harry darling? I did all I could to make you happy and comfortable, my sweetest broad-shouldered Bucha Harry, and so it's not my fault if you did not thoroughly enjoy your holiday and outing, my darling, as I gave you the best I had, viz., myself.

The new powders were too "tasty", and plunged this extraordinary woman into a fit of depression. She put the full dose into the tea which she sent to the office with her husband's tiffin, and he returned the whole jug untasted, and reported to his wife that it was bad, though no inkling of the truth had yet crossed his mind. "Fate is against us," she wails in her letter of the 23rd of May. "The first powders were tasteless, and unsuspected, but not strong enough, but these do not suit at all, darling." Another cause of her depression is the fact which she learns from Clark, that one of her letters has arrived open, and she decides to take his advice and put her postage stamp on the flap of the envelope—a very common device in India. At the same time the "Agra letter-writer" Joseph, seems to have failed to supply Clark with adequate material for some of his more recent letters, and she bursts out with a fit of jealousy:

> My very own precious lovie, don't you think our correspondence rather risky, in case we may be discovered any day? Besides, I do really think you are growing tired, and finding it irksome, for you give me no news whatever, Bucha, darling, but just imitate my letter in return. There seems to be a decided change in you, my own sweetheart, and for the last two days I have been so miserable and unhappy, thinking it all over, darling, I have made myself ill, and so to-day have treated myself to a big dose of oil, which has weakened me.

> Please don't think I need to be "pacified". Oh, no, just leave me to myself; your conversation on Thursday last, Harry darling, has led me to believe that the so-called ladies (God help them to bear the name), you are at present associating with in Agra, are of a very low order. But I will not dictate to you, my Bucha darling, choose for yourself, you must surely agree with me, lovie darling, when one fair dame wishes to go and marry you as she stands? There is lots of news going in Meerut (dear old Meerut, I love it so). But as you refrain from news-telling, so must I refrain, Harry darling. Perhaps the oil has stirred up my liver and made me "moody".

But her fits of jealousy and depression never lasted long, and her next letter is full of passionate assurances, and prayers for his forgiveness. There is a touch of ingenuity as well as humour, about the way in which she subtly leads up to a suggestion for yet another more potent powder:

> Poor old G. is very ill with acute pains in his stomach, Harry darling. He has three doctors attending, enough to kill anyone, I should say, one says gout in the stomach, another says gall-stones, and the third declares it's appendicitis; so let us see between them what they manage to do with the poor man's life, darling. Now this is written with all apologies to my dearest, sweetest darling old Dr Sahib, for, of course, there is none other so clever in my eyes, sweetheart. Harry, darling, as you are so clever, my darling pet, do consider and hit on a plan that will soon achieve our most desired and longed-for results; and darling, if there is anything you wish to send me in a small parcel, please register it.

The account of a wedding which she attended and from which she returned at half-past one in the morning, at the end of May, throws an interesting side-light upon life in Meerut in the hot weather:

> The wedding was a big success, my very own precious darling, and I can tell you their purse must be much lighter after all that expenditure. For my part, I prefer a nice quiet little wedding, to all that display and show, darling. The bride looked most charming and E. looked very happy, but tired. Mr Fullam gave a nice speech. Fancy, Harry darling, the newly married pair are still here in Meerut. They leave to-night for Simla, and I think E. will be very glad to get his bride to himself after so much confusion.

A few days later she returns to the subject of the wedding.

> Now my Bucha, as you express a desire to know with whom I danced at the wedding, I hasten to inform you. I first had a waltz with young Mr V. (do you know him, darling?) The second dance was a set of Lancers, and my partner was a Mr W., a big broad fellow, who reminded me very much of my absent darling, my own precious loved one. This Mr W. asked my hubby why he didn't tell him all this time that there was a Mrs Fullam, and that she was so young and girlish. So my hubby looked at me rather astonished, and said he thought everyone knew Mrs Fullam. What was your first impression, Harry darling, when you first met me? Did you think I was "young and girlish", my own Bucha, lovie darling? I remember worrying Eddie to bring you once, and this is the result, Bucha sweetheart mine.

Towards the end of the month of May, Mr Alick Joseph, the "Agra letter-writer", seems to have woken up, and to have found some soul-stirring lines. Mrs Fullam's sense of humour was aroused, and she says:

The lines at the head or commencement of your dear letter are very uncommon and fine. Now, my own darling, which disease have you got, in the world of love? I should say, neither measles, nor nettle rash, my lovie, but a very serious sickness indeed, from which it appears to me, you will not recover my Bucha pet, what say you, darling?

5
Warnings

The months of June and July were a period of tragedy and of warnings. Mrs Fullam and Clark had a lovers' quarrel through the post. But Clark came over to Meerut to see her on his usual third Thursday, and she spent the day "in a dream of bliss and happiness". He had brought with him a dose of strong poison, and gave it to Mrs Fullam to administer to her husband. The same night the punkah, which swung on cords over her bed, broke and fell upon her, very nearly causing her serious injury. On the next day Mr Fullam had a sudden and violent attack of "heatstroke", which kept him to the house for several days. He suspected that he had been poisoned, and frightened his wife by saying that it was the tiffin. He went away to the Hills on ten days' leave. He evidently heard a good deal about Clark while he was away, and when he learned that Clark had been visiting the house during his absence, he was very angry, and forbade his wife to have him there again. Meanwhile Mrs Fullam, who was an impressionable woman, and moped when she was alone, had passed through a fit of depression. She had been affected by her husband's suffering. She herself suffered from malaria, and a sore tongue. She was haunted by the belief that she was suspected by her husband, and by the evil omen which her superstitious mind harboured about the punkah accident. Faced with the possibility of a termination to her relations with Clark, she grew desperate and impatient, and vacillated between a break with Clark, and a scheme for the prompt murder of her husband. In the midst of all came the inconvenience, and the further evil omen, of an accident to her horse and carriage. Thus Fullam himself was warned that his wife was not to be trusted, his wife received warnings that he was growing suspicious, and was haunted by omens and forebodings, while Clark was warned that matters were approaching a crisis.

But no warnings were capable of quenching their passion for one another, or of damping their ardour. Their separation, and occasional "tiffs" only served to fan the flame. She suffered from Clark's tempers, though she enjoyed his gaiety; she allowed him to bully her, but she seems to have loved him most when she reproached him; she gave him presents, and would not allow him to spend anything upon her; but what were faults in others seemed to her to be almost virtues in him, and though she must often have realized that he would not be an easy man to live with, and that he would be far from an ideal husband, she was at this time prepared to sacrifice everything for him. She lays bare her soul to him in the following passionate letter:

> What was wrong with you to grumble all the letter through and scold your little girl in a way that's astonishing after saying you don't wish to go over the ground again, and then filling your dearest letter with the subject? Harry, darling, my very own precious sweetheart mine, I am sorry I caused you a

moment's heartache or disappointment in not hearing from me. What would you do, if you were to lose me, darling? I do not mean by death, only but even if in this life you never win me, after all, Bucha, what will you do? Suppose I were taken off to England, or some distant part of India. I dread to think of it, my own Bucha darling. Why do you call me heartless and cruel and bearing animosity, Harry dearest, my own precious. I would give my very life for you my Bucha, you should know that. Then why get angry and abuse me, darling, at the same time calling me gentle, generous, and loving hearted? I see we are not finished quarrelling and fighting as yet, Harry darling; but I shall wait until we meet next Thursday, to renew the attack my own darling. I am going to punish you a little more; I will tell you what your punishment is when I am face to face with you, lovie. It won't hurt you very much, dearest love. You know what I mean only too well, my own darling sweetheart.

The visit of the 15th of June took place. Fullam went off as usual to his Masonic dinner. The punishment, no doubt, was inflicted, and a fresh potent poison was handed over by Clark. The next day, having already sent him a "business letter" describing the punkah incident, she wrote to him a second time:

Well my own loving Bucha sweetheart, how did you get through your long journey? I hope your train ran to time, darling, and you had a comfortable night's journey, reaching Agra all safe and in good time for your work lovie? I have already told you all about the nasty accident of last night, which might have ended seriously for me, Harry darling, and then what would you have done, Bucha dearest, for a nice little pet like me? To-day I have a slight headache, and I do miss you so very much, my own precious love. There seems such a blank in my life when you go out of it, darling. The parting was hard and I want you so much. How did you enjoy the whole day and the lovely long twilight drive, darling, and then the walk down "lovers' lane", and all the blissful hours spent together, my own Bucha, dearest? I was in a perfect dream of bliss and happiness, and I yearn for another soon, lovie. Don't reply to my "business" letter here to the house, Harry darling, in case any jealous fancies are roused.

~

I am writing this in the drawing-room, where we have our dining-room table for the sake of the punkah. The dining-room is converted into a bedroom for the punkah too. And my bedroom is empty save for the broken hanging punkah. The excitement of yesterday (Clark's visit) and the shock last night, (the punkah breaking) was too much for me, and the heart attack was dreadful.

This was written before her husband's attack on the Friday night. The next day she writes to announce his serious illness, which began at four o'clock in the morning "with symptoms of cholera". On the 21st she writes complaining that she has been passing through a miserable week. "Do you know," she says, "I have a superstition about that punkah falling down, and I think it's a very bad sign, darling. It still remains just as it fell, and we sleep in the dining-room, and eat in the sitting-room." Her conscience is smiting her. She refers to her birthday—she was thirty-six on the 23rd of June—to which she had been looking forward. "The heat is intense," she says, and adds:

> Harry darling, please don't trouble to send me anything for my birthday, except love and good wishes, I'd rather not, darling, though there is no ill-feeling between us, but why waste money on me, sweetheart? I don't need anything, so that's understood, isn't it, lovie? I am not punishing you. Fondest love and many sweet kisses from your own little sweetheart and Buchee darling.

~

> Mrs Fullam (Snr) sent me a parcel for my birthday this morning. I wish people would leave me alone, I don't want anything, and I don't deserve it.

~

> Oh, Harry, darling, thank you so very much for all your loving, kind and tender wishes for my birthday. Sweetheart, no one is so loving and tender towards me, as you are, Bucha, and it is this quality in dearest self that I prize and value so much, lovie darling. I am so sorry I worried and grieved you about the letter I tore up, which caused you such disappointment, Bucha darling. I am a very wicked girl, am I not? Never mind, on my next birthday I may be solely yours, and then you can kiss me to your heart's content, my sweetie!

The letter she had torn up had been written because she had not heard from him, and in his last letter before the silence he had made a cruel reference to the punkah incident. Her absolute submission to his every whim is, under the circumstances, pathetic:

> I thought you were enjoying your dearest self and were not bothering one bit about me. So I suppose, Harry darling, the

old jealous feelings got the upper hand of poor little Gussie, and my proud spirit rebelled and took refuge in silence, which was more bitter for me than to you, lovie darling. Also, my own darling, to tell you the truth, I was very much hurt and offended because you said that the punkah falling on my head must have caused me to lose my memory. I suppose so, Harry darling.

In the next letter she reports the doctors' opinions about the illness, and continues in a still more passionate strain:

Sweetheart mine, you wish to know if he has "been near me at all". Well, yes, darling, we are quite friendly and have never quarrelled, even after Friday's affair. He has taken me in his arms once or twice, to relieve his feelings, Harry darling. You know exactly how I mean, lovie. But it makes no difference to me because I think of you all the time. I thoroughly enjoy you and have you for my very own, Harry lovie. You can be quite sure when you get me, that you are the only one who really *does* get me properly, and so I am always yours, and only yours, darling.

~

Sweetheart mine, you will say "what a very strange girl this Gussie of mine is," when you read the P.S. which is longer than my letter, and so full of red-hot sentiments, lovie. Sweetheart darling, if my hubby leaves on Saturday evening, then on Sunday you can address your dearest letter here to me, until his return, Bucha, I may send Frank up with him, not certain yet. So only "Carrots" (Myrtle), and I will be left, my little "mixture of copper and tin". She's a sweet little thing. Darling, now goodbye, I love writing to you, lovie,

> you are the only one who loves me truly and devotedly. God
> bless and keep you, Harry darling.

It was arranged that Fullam should have ten days' leave to recoup. This he decided to spend at Mussoorie, perhaps the most beautiful and interesting hill station in India. He was to start on Saturday night from Meerut and spend Sunday with his brother, William Fullam, in Dehra Dun, the railway terminus, another charming spot, full of verdure, and pleasant shade, lying in the centre of the Doon, at the foot of the hills. Those who have visited Mussoorie in clear weather will remember the glorious view from the Mall looking down on the plains 7,000 or 8,000 feet below, and the lights of Dehra Dun after sunset sparkling in the distance like fairyland. The two brothers had not met since their visit to England six years before. It was to be their last meeting. William's serious illness was a source of great anxiety to his brother Edward when the latter was lying in hospital during September suffering from his last "heatstroke", and he died just a week before his brother's end. Mrs Fullam announces the programme to Clark, while enclosing a tiny little photo of "my sweet smiling face", for his locket, which he is to wear but not to let anyone see. Her cold-blooded treachery at this moment seems almost incredible. Her husband was forced to take sick-leave, and she continued to put powdered arsenic daily in his Sanatogen.

> I don't think my hubby regards you as an enemy, but as a
> friend and Masonic brother, just the same. He has never
> mentioned your name since you were here last, darling
> Bucha, and after all, it may only be imagination on my part
> that he suspected me.

Clark, the irrepressible, declares his intention of not letting "the grass grow under his feet", but of coming over by the next mail to stay at Meerut. Mrs Fullam discourages the idea, and tells him that she cannot possibly come to the station at midnight to meet him. Clark, with his usual selfish impetuosity, loses his temper over this. Mrs Fullam again shows what a child she was in his hands, and what a naturally sweet disposition she had. She writes:

> Sweetheart mine, I am not disappointed that you cannot come to Meerut just at present, but rather glad, my own Bucha, because I think it will look much better for servants and friends, and all, if you come a few days after and not immediately hubby's back is turned. So "everything happens for the best", Harry darling, don't you agree with me, lovie? We will make up for the time lost, won't we, lovie? I am sorry to see such a dash of temper in your dearest letter, when I think you might have been more reasonable, darling, about my coming to the station to meet you, as you must know and realize perfectly well that it is a hard, nay, almost impossible thing to do. I did it once before, I am quite aware, darling, but you know how risky it was, and how I was seen by young E.

Clark eventually came on the 5th and stayed four days, "those four blissful days", she calls them. It was the time of the rains, and they spent much of the day in the bungalow, reading aloud to one another. "Neither of us can ever forget those happy hours and days together, nor do we wish to forget them, my own darling." And she quotes some lines from a book she is reading:

> Thenceforth in dreams must we each other's shadows see,
> Wandering unsatisfied in empty lands;
> Still the desired face
> Fleets from the vain embrace;
> And still the hands evade the longing hands.

On the 11th of July she announces that her husband is returning, and that they cannot afford to take any risks. This seems to have made her momentarily desperate. She is still "wandering unsatisfied in empty lands", and she is struck with the brilliant idea of despatching her husband by less tedious methods than those of Clark's, and by a bold stroke, which is henceforth to be known as the "heatstroke". Although she knew nothing of the contents and effects of this mixture there is little doubt that she was the original author of the idea. There is something piquant about the suggestion that while this fate is to be artificially produced upon her husband, her lover should take precautions to avoid the same catastrophe to himself from natural causes:

> Harry, my very own precious sweetheart, I must mention to you that Mr N. got a heatstroke. There was a death of Col. B. of heat apoplexy in the train at Ghazibad, darling, so it's always safe for you to travel at night and not in the day, my own Bucha.

Mr Fullam's very natural perturbation and indignation when he heard from his wife that Clark had been visiting Meerut during his absence in the Hills precipitated matters. On the 14th July Mrs Fullam writes:

> Harry, darling, my very own precious, dearest love, it is with a very sad heart indeed that I am writing to you to-day. I

The Story of the Crime 61

told you in yesterday's letter that we were walking as lovers on the verge of a precipice. Well, my darling, the ground has given way beneath our feet, and now we are hurled into the abyss below. But I am writing in parables, sweetheart darling, and to be more explicit I must tell you plainly that my hubby had a good row with me last evening, and spoke very plainly to me, forbidding me to have anything more to do with you, lovie. He is very angry that you brought me the shoes, Bucha darling, and also that you came to see me while he was away. He has also noticed that you come regularly on the third Thursday of every month, sweetie, and he expects to see you turn up again next week when he intends to speak plainly to you, darling. So please do not come to Meerut now, I cannot write and tell you, darling, all that took place during the row, but some day perhaps I shall tell you all. Oh! God, when will the day dawn when I shall see dearest self again? I am locking up the shoes, because it's no use making matters worse by wearing them, the very sight of them makes him furious, he says you are making me obligated to you, darling, and trying to win me away from him. He also said that if he thought there was anything between us, he would shoot me first with a revolver, and then shoot himself. So you see, my own Bucha darling, what a state matters have come to, and how we must now decide at once and for ever, whether we will part or whether we will sacrifice everything to be together, dearest love. The only thing that keeps me back from doing it, my Bucha darling, is the thought of ways and means, and how to manage afterwards, for you know how proud I am, and would never touch a pice offered from relatives, or anybody else, darling. Do you think I could get the Masons to educate, or help me to educate Leonard? All those and many other thoughts keep worrying your dearest

> little Buchee night and day, lovie, and sometimes I feel very down-hearted and ill. I look stout and well, Bucha darling, but oh, my heart is sick and heavy within me. He has taken me in his arms, lovie, you know how I mean, more than once…. He has come back much stronger and better, and this makes it very difficult for your little girlie, Henry darling.
>
> He came back from Dehra evidently prejudiced against you very much, and as I mentioned that you were here last Saturday he became very jealous, and told me you were a very bad man, and warned me to have nothing to do with you in future, sweetheart.

Another omen occurred to depress the superstitious little woman. Their horse fell and cut his knees, and broke the shafts of the phaeton. Mrs Fullam had a fit of hysterics. Meanwhile the "green-eyed monster" was gnawing at the heart of Fullam. In accordance with her warning, Clark did not come over to Meerut as usual the third Thursday in the month. It was the night of Fullam's Masonic Lodge dinner, and his wife was not surprised, but was at the same time disturbed, by his arriving home unexpectedly, much earlier than his wont. He found her sitting with a lady friend whom she had met in the course of a lonely walk taken to relieve her mind from the depression caused by Clark's absence. Her overmastering passion, her despair, and her determination to get rid of her husband, were all combining to urge her on to strong measures. Her interest in the objective consequences of the forthcoming dose, and her anxiety to be able to recognize the symptoms, disclose the morbid condition of her mind at this time. She asks her lover:

> Harry, lovie, please let me know by return of post (the mixture had not even arrived), if in the heatstroke treatment,

> the face will become perfectly black and distorted and convulsions set in? Will you please let me know if it will be a very painful death, or will unconsciousness soon intervene? Also, my darling, please let me know if I can administer the liquid at dinner time, or tea time? Which do you think will be the best, darling? You see, it will be so hard for me to get a doctor, or anybody to help me at night, whereas broad daylight is so much easier. I only hope that no suspicion will point to me, Harry darling!

All this reads cold-blooded indeed, and yet so superfluous, because in her then state of determination nothing could suit her purpose better, or be more likely to avert the growth of suspicion against her than the impossibility of obtaining medical aid. It is a tragic coincidence that while she was soon to learn the terrible results of Clark's "heatstroke" mixture, she was also to learn, by personal experience, the symptoms of heatstroke from natural causes, for it was this which terminated her own life, two years afterwards, when she was nursing her baby in Naini Jail. The following extracts from another of her letters written about this time show the phases through which her mind was passing:

> Why do you want me, lovie darling? There are nicer, better and more good people than I, in this world, my very own precious sweetie. Oh, Harry darling, since you went away I have not had a strong arm round me, or a strong arm like yours, to lean upon, I am so lonely and heart-sick, lovie Bucha. Never mind, I will be brave and carry out this scheme of ours until the end, my own darling, all for your sake, and because I love you so devotedly and passionately. You will never know how much I love you, Bucha—sweetheart mine.

What would you advise me to do? Should I stay in Meerut, in a cheaper house, or leave it for a smaller and cheaper station, darling? What about your part of the business? How would you free your dearest self of Mrs C.? Surely you would not offer me any less position than that of wife.

Oh, Harry darling, how much I love you! This proves my fond, devoted, passionate and earnest love for you, in trying to please you, darling, in every way. You should never in all your life forget such love as this, because you will get no one else to love you so, darling sweetie, my Bucha. You must not attempt to free yourself so soon as next month, as it will look very bad in the eyes of the world, darling, and you have grown-up children, who might notice your anxiety to become a widower as soon as Mrs Fullam is alone in the world. No, my sweetheart, I will wait for you, as I told you, lovie, and will marry no one else, darling. I will be your future dear, little brown-haired, blue-eyed wifie darling, and I only mentioned Mr H., just to worry and make you jealous, my own loving Bucha.

On the 22nd of July she wrote one of the most remarkable of the whole series of her love letters:

Saturday, July 22nd

My Ever Dearest, Very Own Precious, Harry Sweetheart, Bucha Darling,

Your most loving, kind and welcome letter, dated Friday, 21st, reached my hands quite safely from the P.O., through the coachman, my own darling. Thanks many for the same, Bucha lovie. You request me to be sure and send you a few pencilled lines, darling, which I cannot promise to do to-morrow, being Sunday, Bucha, but you know I will do my best and try and not disappoint you, my very own precious darling, my own love.

~

Mrs T. and her two sisters came over this morning and sat chatting from breakfast time until 12.30, and they have only just gone, lovie darling. So I have sat down late to write my usual letter, darling. Sweetheart, darling, my lady friends all say that Mrs Fullam is so nice and agreeable and kind that they love to stay here with me, and not go away. We had tea and biscuits and some music and song, Harry darling.

~

Harry sweetheart, my very own precious lovie darling, don't trouble to send me the book of pictures you write and tell me of, I shall see it some day when I am near you, darling, and just now I don't care to see things like that, my mind is filled with other subjects. Why do you keep a book of that description, Harry dear? It only excites the mind and passions, and is not good or wholesome in any way, Bucha. My hubby has read through the Sexual Science since his return, sweetheart, but it makes no difference to him. He has his own way and style of doing things. I told him I was a padmani (spiritually minded) woman; not to forget that; and he said I was a little goose, my own darling.

Harry darling, my own precious lovie Bucha, you can send me the heatstroke liquid, as you say, next week, and I shall see what can be done, dearest love. After I am once free, I shall curtail my expenses, Harry Bucha, perhaps leaving Meerut. Then I shall live very quietly alone, until next March, after I send Leonard and Katty up to school to the hills, darling. I shall wait for you, my sweetie, until the middle of March, so that you will have ample time to free yourself and get ready, in case you may wish to change your mind, lovie. I daresay both Mr H. and S. may wish to have me, if possible, but if I don't marry you, Harry darling, then I shall marry no one else.

Fondest, warmest, truest and never-changing love and many millions of sweetest, loving kisses from your own true, constant-loving, best-beloved and most devoted little sweetheart and Buchee darling.

Gussie
Till death.

Try and be a good boy, for my sake, lovie. That book won't help you much!

This letter is remarkable, not only for what it contains, but for what it ignores, and for the proof it affords of the fundamental inconsistency, even in her innermost thoughts and in her most intimate relations, of this strange woman. It is certain that Clark was coarse and sensual, and delighted in indecent literature. It is equally certain that Mrs Fullam had a strain of spirituality and decency in her character, and a leaning towards religion, which was never wholly absent from her mind, even during her most criminal activities. And yet there were letters found in the collection which she wrote to Clark of so intimate and indecent a character that the police decided to suppress them as being both superfluous and unfit for publication.

6
In the Toils

Before the end of July the die was cast, and the crisis in this extraordinary story of deceit and crime was rapidly approaching. There had been difficulties about fetching Clark's letters from the Post Office, owing to the accident to the horse and trap. But at last the shaft had been promised, and she would be able to drive out and fetch things for herself. So she writes on July the 24th:

> You are impatient to send me the liquid, darling, and so am I—very impatient to get through with this whole business—which is weighing very heavily on my spirits, Bucha lovie, as you may well imagine. But I think you had better wait until Wednesday, the 26th, darling, and then send it to me, so that I can call for it, and I shall disguise my signature, as you so wisely suggest.
>
> ~
>
> Regarding the prescription for drops, I am going to comply with your dearest wish for once, because I think in your great eagerness to win me, darling, you might injure his eyes and perhaps blind him, and so the last case will be worse than the first. Now, please don't be offended at the above statement, my own darling, for you are the cleverest, dearest, kindest doctor that I know, but I mean in your great love for me, you might only hurt his eyes, and yet not rid ourselves of his presence, darling.

Can human ingenuity conceive a more startling mixture of criminal infatuation and callousness in a woman who was of gentle disposition, sweet and affectionate by nature, and respected and admired by her friends? She had written the day before to explain her plan of campaign. On the 29th she received the bottle of poison through the post. The story of its arrival, and of the workings of her mind as she approached her grim task, is best told in her own graphic language:

> Your kind and loving letter dated Wednesday, 26th, together with the small parcel containing the heatstroke liquid, reached me quite safely at the P.O. this morning. Many thanks, lovie darling, for the same. How very nicely you have packed the box, Harry darling! And I recognized the family seal and crest on the sealing wax. The mixture arrived quite safe and sound with not one drop spilt, lovie, and when I opened the little scent box, I did as you desired, darling, and put one tiny drop on my tongue to taste. Oh, Harry darling, it's very bitter, in spite of your lime-juice and salt! I thought you said it would be a white, colourless liquid, like water, my darling. But it's yellow, thick, sticky and bitter. I suppose the added lime-juice has coloured it yellow? Now, Harry darling, I know you have done your very best. So that if it is God's good will, he will make all our efforts come to a successful issue, and if not, then we must part, sweetie darling, and think no more of each other. We cannot go on very much longer as we are doing, lovie Bucha, as things are getting harder for us.
>
> I am sure when he tastes his plate of soup this evening at dinner, he will remark that it tastes like bad medicine, darling, the same that he complained of the jallap. Anyhow, I shall try unless anything happens to prevent me. If I am successful, I shall send you just a line, letting you know the results. I shall certainly not send you a wire, as you don't wish it. You can't expect much news from me to-morrow, if we are crowned with success, but I shall let you know, lovie darling.

To-day is an exceptionally hot day, Harry darling, just the exact weather for heatstroke. I am very glad to hear that you are quite well again, my lovie, and I pray that God will richly bless you in all your life, even if you may never win me after all, sweetie. This is really a crisis in both our lives, my own Bucha darling, and I only wonder how it will end, sweetheart?

Fondest, warmest, truest and never-changing love, and many millions of sweetest loving kisses, from your own true, constant-loving, best-beloved and most devoted, little sweetheart and Buchee darling.

Gussie

Till death, no matter what happens.

~

Friday, July 28th

They have taken away my dear hubby to the hospital, after a most dreadful night, more like a nightmare.

I have a very severe headache, being up all night, and being so upset. I feel heartbroken, and only wish to die. Would that I were never born, as I am so wicked.

He seemed to recognize my voice at the head of his bed, though he never saw me. But he patted the orderly's cheek and said, "My dear little girl, you have come to see me. How are the kiddies?"

~

Saturday, July 29th

Harry lovie, my own precious sweetheart, I have a great disappointment in store for you, but evidently it is God's will to spare my hubby's life, and he is not going to die, Bucha darling.

~

> Sunday, July 30th
>
> My ever-dearest, very own precious Harry sweetheart, Bucha darling, many thanks for your loving, kind and most welcome letter of sweet sympathy to hand safely this morning. I must confess that I do feel very sad and miserable to think I am the cause of so much suffering and expense to one who has never done me any harm in all his or my life, but only loved me tenderly.
>
> Oh, Harry darling, I feel lonely, sad, downhearted, dull and utterly unhappy and wretched. When my hubby leaves hospital, he is going up to Mussoorie I think, but he told me this morning he would not go without me and the children. Just imagine all the expense, and how can I leave the house and live-stock, and specially you, my own pet, lovie darling?
>
> This last attempt has proved a dead failure, and means a lot of extra expense and trouble, no wonder my heart is sick within me, what with great disappointment and worry, lovie. They say "Hope deferred maketh the heart sick", my Bacha darling.
>
> So you see, everything points plainly that we must part and forget each other, although Heaven knows it will be sore and sorry work, my own lovie, darling, my heart's own precious treasure.
>
> You don't blame me at all, do you, darling? I have been very brave and have done my best, but fate wills it otherwise, and we must each do our duty where God has placed us, my Bucha darling. They have diagnosed my hubby's case as heatstroke, lovie darling, and no one has the slightest suspicion of the truth, my own lovie.

Whatever feeling of regret Mrs Fullam had at this time was due entirely to the failure of the plot. She certainly had been "brave", but, fatalistic as ever, she does not show any special signs of relief on finding that there was not "the slightest suspicion of the truth". How this came about is a medical question which has no place in this historical chapter. Clark's expressions of sympathy with her distress seem almost farcical in their impudence, but they evidently did not strike Mrs Fullam as being in the least unnatural. Clark must have been a fairly shrewd and long-sighted criminal, if he had had no previous practice. There were rumours afterwards that Fullam was not his first victim, as Mrs Fullam was certainly not his first capture. It is as certain as anything can be that if it had not been for Clark's foresight Mrs Fullam would have announced her husband's attack by sending a wire to Clark at Agra, and it is possible that if she had done so there might have been talk in Meerut, where Mrs Fullam's secret correspondence was well known to the employees at the post office.

Mr Fullam was liked and respected in his office, both by his superiors and by those who worked under him. The authorities decided that when he got better he should go off on medical leave for three months. While he was in hospital the Controller telegraphed each day inquiring about his condition, and the office staff showed Mrs Fullam great kindness and sympathy, and offered her every sort of assistance. She herself speaks of this in her letters to Clark. Although the attentions which Clark had been paying for some time to Mrs Fullam had attracted notice, he was well known to be a "Don Juan", and he was a man so inferior in every way to Fullam, and Mrs Fullam was so discreet in her conduct, particularly in public, that until Fullam's death after his departure from Meerut, their friends took very little notice of what was going on.

The idea of Fullam going away on sick leave was abandoned. He left hospital on August the 14th. Mrs Fullam thought that the doctors were making a mistake in allowing him back so soon. He was normal, but it was very hot, and she thought there was a risk of a relapse. It was Clark's birthday, and her birthday letter to him shows a chastened mood, and strongly suggests that she had made up her mind that the recent failure was to be the end of the attempts they had been making on her husband's life. "You are obliged to keep very quiet," she writes, "and do things you would otherwise never do, and that is, control your feelings and temper, darling, and let things rest just to please me, and I know you will."

At this stage there are considerable breaks in the correspondence. No effort seems to have been made to fill up the gaps with direct evidence at the trial, or it may be that it was thought unnecessary in view of the overwhelming evidence, and of the admissions which had been made by the culprits. Nothing could stem the tide of Clark's iniquity, though it is uncertain whether he really preferred Mrs Fullam to his other lady friends, of whose existence Mrs Fullam shows, even in her birthday letter to him, that she was well aware. It is certain that he came over to Meerut to see Mr Fullam on the latter's return to his bungalow, probably on Wednesday, August the 16th, instead of on his usual third Thursday. On this Thursday Mr Fullam was probably given the second dose of "heatstroke" mixture. It is unlikely, from what one knows of Clark's character and cunning, that he would have allowed another dose to be given while he was in Meerut, particularly as he had no business which would account for his presence in the Station. The only reason for his visits was to see the Fullams. Nor is it likely that he brought with him another bottle. There is no reference in the letters written by Mrs Fullam about her husband's return from hospital to any expected visit from Clark. Nor is there any suggestion of administering another dose. And whatever they did, or proposed to do, was always fully discussed beforehand by Mrs Fullam in her letters. There is the further observation to be made, that Clark would have very little time to prepare a fresh bottle, and very little opportunity for handing it to Mrs Fullam while Mr Fullam and the children were in the bungalow, without running the risk of attracting notice. We know that the remains of the first bottle had been put away in a cupboard, and that little Myrtle eventually in September got hold of it and sucked the cork, and that in spite of this Mrs Fullam told Clark in one of her letters that she would only throw it away in his presence. It is probable, nay, almost certain, that Clark came to see Mr Fullam on the Wednesday. Mrs Fullam, who told several falsehoods in her confession, in an effort to save herself, pretended that she knew nothing about this second dose. Her letters show conclusively that she did. She said in her confession that during these days Clark did come over and was alone with her husband. It is absurd to suppose that Clark could have given this dose. It would have been none of his business, and Mr Fullam was taking regular medicine which had been prescribed for him, while the "heatstroke" mixture was particularly unpleasant. This dose must have been given by Mrs Fullam herself at the incident related at the trial by little Kathleen and set out in Chapter III, p. 132.

Captain Weston, a retired officer of the I.S.M.D., said at the trial that he was sent for about 4 p.m., and found Mr Fullam in a very serious condition, gasping the words, "hospital, hospital". He thought his life was in immediate danger and sent him straight back to hospital again. It appeared to him to be a case of another "heatstroke", for which the wife had fully prepared the doctors. Again no suspicion was aroused. But Mr Fullam's condition was more serious, and the hospital authorities were satisfied that he would never again be fit for work. He remained in hospital until the 7th of October, when his wife and Clark took him to Agra. During the stay in hospital Clark made more frequent visits to Meerut, and from this time his correspondence was addressed direct to where Mrs Fullam was living.

On Saturday, the 2nd of September, the Medical Board sat on the case, and decided that Fullam was no longer fit for work and that he must retire. The Fullams were offered a free passage to England on a troopship, a *denouement* which caused Mrs Fullam unmixed distress. Her letters show how the proposal affected her mind. Later on Fullam himself decided, doubtless under the persuasive influence of his wife, to retire and live in India. Mrs Fullam for the next few weeks was engaged in disposing of the furniture and carriage, of course at a serious sacrifice, as everyone acquainted with life in an Indian Station can understand, particularly at such an unpromising season as the middle of the rains. The interest of the remaining letters centres upon the discussion of these alternative plans, and the sudden and fatal decision of Fullam himself, whom nothing would induce to return to his old residence, to move to Agra, where Clark had obtained a bungalow for them, at No. 9, Metcalfe Road. When the retirement to England seemed to be the most probable outcome Mrs Fullam wrote the following letter. The suggestion in the graphological allusion is an indication of the bent of her thoughts:

> Your kind, loving and welcome letter to hand safely this morning, for which many thanks, darling. It is only one of the few more letters I shall receive from my sweetest treasure, and then never more will I see the dear, familiar handwriting with its firm, upward strokes, so determined and so characteristic of the beloved writer, darling!
>
> What a shame that we two, who love each other so devotedly and passionately must part, perhaps never to meet again in this wide world, lovie. Oh, it cannot be, it is not possible, surely. The blue sky and flowers during day, and the moon and stars by night, would all be darkness and chaos without your dear presence, Harry darling, my one and only love, my King.
>
> There is no more to say, Bucha. You are coming soon to see me, to-night you will be here, I shall see your dear face, touch your hands and face, and see you smile. But all that will make it so much harder! Oh, God give me strength to bear this cruel, bitter blow of disappointment and parting, after all I have done. It is not my fault, Harry dearie, it is simply fate. I cannot write more. Much fond love from your loving little sweetheart and Buchee darling.
>
> Gussie
(Till death).

On Sunday, the 3rd of September, she writes:

> I should never have made such an attempt on his poor life, which has resulted in cruel disappointment and wrecking of his whole nervous system, brain and all. Sweetheart mine,

he can't even sign his pay bill, and so I can get no money this month.

The woman's kittenish playfulness comes out even in the midst of her worry and distress:

> Lovie, to-day is Katty's ninth birth anniversary, and she thanks you very much for your nice, kind little letter to her enclosed in mine. She is quite pleased with it, and desires her love and thanks. But certainly you must not send her anything as a present, my own Bucha darling, unless you wish to displease me very much indeed, then you can do as you like, but I tell you what, my darling, if you really wish to give her a present, let me give her a bottle of scent which you so kindly gave me, darling, and I can say that you sent it for her, while she was at school, and then afterwards you can replace it to me, if it so pleases you.

Then came the agony:

> Bucha, lovie pet, you will be sorry to hear that the Board sat yesterday on my hubby's case, and have decided to grant him and his family, of wife and four children, a free passage home to England, sailing either from Bombay or Karachi by the second or third Troopship, which will mean leaving India by the end of October. Now I am sure this is the very worst news I could possibly give you, Harry darling, my own Bucha sweetie, but you know I am tied down to do whatever my hubby and his doctors advise, so I can't act as I wish. You should have made quite certain and sure of everything in that one dose, my lovie darling, if you wanted me so much, and now I am afraid there will never be another chance to do the same thing over again, as he has a perfect dread and horror of this house, lovie darling, and begs and asks not to

be brought here again. So I suppose he will go straight away from the hospital or something like that, my lovie. Of course I feel all this very much, and am worried. But if it is your fate and mine to be parted, darling, then nothing on earth can help it, Bucha pet.

I have been very busy and sat up last night making out a list of property for "sale of E.M. Fullam, Esq., proceeding home." I never bargained for all this trouble and worry, when I made that third and last attempt, as you led me to believe sweetheart, for I fully thought and believed, that all would turn out satisfactorily, and that you, darling, would be a help and a support to me in all things. But now, I am left all alone to use my own brains and to help myself, having neither my husband nor my own darling lover, to help or comfort me. I suppose it really serves me right, and it's making me very bitter towards the world in general, my own darling.

I sympathize deeply with you, darling, in losing me whom your loving heart has grown to love and worship so much, but I am helpless and powerless, you know that, lovie. I pray that God will always bless, guard and keep you.

With my heart's warmest, fondest and truest love and many millions of sweetest, loving kisses from your own true, constant, best-beloved and dearest little sweetheart and Buchee darling.

Gussie
(Till death).

My darling, be brave and ask God to hear us both in this dark hour of parting.

She complains to him again that events have turned out quite differently from what they expected, and from "what you led me to believe." She tells him to go off and love someone else, but adds, with a touch of that womanly vanity which never left her, that she knows he never will. It was willed otherwise. About this time another omen happened. "A bat fell on him from the roof last night," she writes, "and gave him such a start, I wonder if that means anything, lovie darling, as you know I am very superstitious." On the 6th September she writes:

> I was so surprised, lovie darling, to read the very first item in your enclosed future foretold. As it says you will soon have an important letter giving you news of my change of residence. Well, here it is, the important letter, and now wouldn't you like to know where your little Buchee darling is off to? What fun it would be, if you lost me even in Meerut, my darling? Shall I tell you, lovie? Well, I have taken two rooms at the Dak Bungalow, and am very busy shifting over there, Bucha. I shall live quietly for the month or so that my hubby is still detained in hospital, lovie darling, and after that we shall go away somewhere, to a nice, quiet cheap place in India, not England, as they have decided that my hubby must take pension if he goes to England, otherwise we do not get a free passage, darling. So he has no desire or wish to go to England, and neither have I. He is talking of settling down in Bangalore or some other nice place, but there is nothing at all definite, Bucha pet.

~

> I can't write any more now, and what is the use of my writing again? My husband is very ill, I am the only one allowed to see him, he never speaks to me hardly, but just lies with his eyes closed. He can't walk as you suppose, nor can he even sit up, but just twitches and jumps, and in the intervals stares like a lunatic.

What a prospect! But I did it, and so I deserve a ruined life and a broken home, and no friends and no comforts.

~

Another thing that has turned my very soul, and made me bitter towards the whole world in general, darling, is the scandal which from time to time reaches my ears—I don't like to repeat all I hear to you, Bucha, for you naturally get very angry, and so I have to bear all my troubles alone and in silence, which, as you say "eats into the very soul", and makes life so hard to bear.

~

How you do beg and plead to be reinstated in my tender loving heart, Harry darling! What am I to say? You are a man to talk any one over, most of all poor little me, who although very forgiving and sweet and loving at times, can also change completely and be cold, bitter, hard, merciless. You know my true nature well, darling. You have not studied me for two long years in vain, and not to know that I am a very peculiar little person, very proud and distant at times (when jealousy grows) and most loving in ordinary surroundings.

~

No young lady could ever so eagerly expect her daily love letters as I do, my darling pet, and I am more disappointed. But oh, Harry, sweetheart, this is all wrong, because you have your lawful wife, and I have my hubby, so it's that which worries me so, darling. I am so glad to hear my precious darling sweet is well, but you must not give way to sorrow or grief on my account, lovie pet. Please do not think of such an awful thing as a fatal dose for dearest self, should you love me for ever, darling. I know you are a brave, strong man, my own dearest soldier doctor, but it's only cowards who find a way out of life.

~

I wish you were not so madly in love with me, I really think you can smother all your passionate love, but you are such a headstrong determined man, my own darling. You are determined to win your little Buchee at any cost. I am sorry to say that Mr H. has also fallen in love with me, darling, but like a wise man he keeps away and does not come near temptation. He is a good chap, has been ill lately with dysentery, I shall tell you all and hide nothing when we meet, darling.

It had been decided after all that the Fullams should go to Dehra Dun and join Willie Fullam who was very seriously ill. Saturday, October 7th, had been fixed for the departure, and the ayah was to precede them with the children on the Friday. And then, suddenly, strangest event of all in this eventful history, Mr Fullam decided to go to Agra. The decision is announced in a letter to Clark of the 3rd of October:

Lovie, dearest, you seem to be quite perplexed by my wire of yesterday afternoon, and I am sorry I worried you so. But I did get excited hearing about Willie Fullam's death, and then my hubby's sudden decision to go to Agra, that I rushed off and sent you that wire. I hope and trust you received my letter of explanation, my own darling, and I wonder if you can secure that little place in Metcalfe Road for us?

Sweetheart mine, I feel sure you will try and get a nice suitable place in Agra, because you would like immensely to have me near you, and this is such a good chance when he is so eager to go to Agra for a change during the winter months, darling. On hearing from you I shall write and decide about the house in Dehra Dun. If we can't go to Agra, we will go there.

7
Death

What caused Mr Fullam to decide to go to Agra? This is one of the mysteries in this terrible story which can never be cleared up. It was a sudden decision. We have seen that arrangements had been made for a house at Dehra Dun, and that the ayah was to take the children there on the Friday. One would be inclined to think, at first sight, that Mrs Fullam had managed to persuade her husband against his will. He was in a pitiably weak state of health. He was an upright man, of gentle disposition. Although he exercised his marital authority sufficiently to make his wife afraid of him, and anxious not to cross him, he did not fight much against her wayward nature. His mind had by this time given way under the influence of the deadly poison in his system, and he was past his work. Mrs Fullam was showing him every sign of affection and sympathy. The orderly, Gunner Dixon, said at the trial that during her visits to hospital they were very happy together, and the suffering man seemed to want to have her with him. She was a clever woman, and had great power of persuasion. He was just in the condition most likely to be amenable to any pressure which she desired to bring to bear upon him. Yet there is no evidence that she did so in order to persuade him to choose Agra. There is a good deal against it. She made Clark her confidant in every step she took, even about her children, and there is not a word of it in her letters. On the contrary she announced it as a great surprise, by telegram, and confirmed it by letter, and in the whole of her relationship with Clark there is not a trace of her ever having told him a falsehood, unless this is the one exception.

One thing is made quite certain by her communications to Clark. Whatever efforts he had made from time to time to persuade Mr Fullam to settle down in retirement in Agra, he had nothing to do with the final decision. Gunner Dixon evidently thought that it was entirely the doing of Clark. His evidence at the trial makes this abundantly clear. He said:

> Clark more than once suggested that he should go to Agra. He used to come alone to see Fullam at the hospital. They both used to suggest to him that it would be good for his health to go to Agra. Before he left the hospital he knew that he was going to Agra. He told me so more than once. I remember him telling me that he thought Clark had given him poison. He did not want to go there. He said to me when we were alone that if he went to Agra he would be poisoned. He did not name anyone. I had my own ideas, so did not ask him.

The witness also added that when he was with the Fullams in the dak bungalow, and again at the station, Fullam told him, when the other two were out of hearing, that he did not want to go to Agra. Some of this evidence must be taken *cum grano salis*. They may have tried to talk Fullam over into going. But the witness admitted that he had said not a word to the doctors, either that Fullam thought he had been poisoned, or that he thought he would be poisoned if he went to Agra, or even that he did not want to go to Agra at all. His explanation was that "patients tell us all sorts of things and we have to take no notice of what they say." This is, no doubt, true, but if the whole of his evidence is true, it was a very serious matter, of which he had some support under his very eyes, and a mere whisper to one of the doctors would have sufficed. If we still accept the view that Mrs Fullam did not lie to Clark there is one further piece of evidence that the choice, strange as it may seem, and fatal, suicidal, though it turned out to be, was the choice of Fullam himself. Mrs Fullam says in one of her letters to Clark: "We must be very careful not to make my hubby jealous, darling, as he may take it into his head to leave Agra."

As for Fullam himself, though he may have had reason to distrust Clark as a man, and as an admirer of his wife, and may have had occasional pangs of jealousy, he believed in Clark as a doctor, and firmly believed that he had once saved the life of Mrs Fullam and Myrtle. He no doubt thought that he was able to look after his own wife in Agra, even better than he had done in Meerut, because now he would be in retirement, devoting his whole time to his family and to his garden, with such home work of accountancy for private persons as he could manage to pick up. Moreover, if he thought over the matter deeply, whatever games Clark might be up to when he paid his fleeting visits to Meerut, in Agra he would have his wife and family, and also his official position, to think of, and these things would tend to keep him quiet. So that on the whole the position would be distinctly better in Agra than in Meerut. And there we must be content to leave the matter.

Mr Fullam knew quite well that Clark was assisting Mrs Fullam in arranging for the journey, and in finding the house at Agra, and the installation when they got there. This was Mrs Clark's business if it was anyone's, though even that gentle soul would probably have found some excuse for shirking it. But this point did not occur to Fullam, or, if it did, he was content to leave it to his wife to arrange. She arranged extraordinarily well. She made Clark work like a nigger, covering him with loving phrases the while, and one wonders what happened to his work at the hospital, and to his patients. Fullam even sent messages explaining the kind of easy chair which he liked. This part of Mrs Fullam's correspondence shows her to have been a methodical and energetic little woman, and a clever housewife, with plenty of foresight. One of the only letters we have of Clark's, to which the "Agra letter-writer" could hardly have contributed, contains much detail about furniture, and fulsome expressions of love, obviously copied from the abundant vocabulary which Mrs Fullam so generously lavished upon him. Clark came to Meerut on the Saturday, and at 6 p.m. Mr Fullam was moved from hospital to the dak bungalow. He had to be carried by Dixon. Mrs Fullam's bearer swore at the trial that he was able to walk supported on either side by his wife and Clark. But this was obviously only a sample of the false testimony with which most Indian witnesses embellish the truth, when they can be induced to tell the truth at all, on those occasions when they have mastered the theory which the police desire to establish. Gunner Dixon said quite simply that Fullam was unable to walk from sheer weakness, and that he had to be given brandy in the dak bungalow, but that otherwise he did not appear to be in any way dangerously ill. Much the same condition seems to have continued after his arrival at Agra. He arrived there on the early morning of Sunday, the 8th. According to Kathleen, he seemed better, and not in the least likely to die. The evening of the 10th was hot. He was sitting in the garden outside the bungalow, and had his dinner there, while Mrs Fullam and Clark dined in the dining room with the children. It is certain that his wife put poison in his food again. She brought his soup and his meat from the cookhouse, with her own hand, a point which seemed to impress the bearer. Indian servants seldom understand anybody waiting on others, or even on himself, being themselves unwilling to do anything which they can get anyone else to do for them. In the middle of his dinner Mr Fullam got up and went into his room to lie down. It was for the last time, and his worn-out frame was approaching its final rest and respite from suffering. Clark actually boasted at the trial that he had put him out of his misery. Mr Fullam vomited as usual, and called out. Clark went to him. Mrs Fullam studiously kept away, and did not see him again alive. Kathleen went to bed but she could see what was going on. She saw Clark go to a table in a corner of the room, and prepare something with a syringe, then, bending over the bed, apply the syringe to her father. She thought he was doing something cruel, but it was really the most merciful thing Clark ever did. Clark sent the bearer off to the club to find Captain Dunne. Soon after the bearer had gone Clark came into the dining-room where Mrs Fullam was and uttered the single word, "Gone". Mrs Fullam, in her confession, said that her husband, when dying, asked Clark to look after his wife and children.

Mrs Fullam took the news quietly, and did not enter the room. Probably this was due partly to superstitious fear, as well as to indifference, but it was not lost upon Kathleen. Her father's sufferings had drawn her very near to him and away from her mother, whom she thought callous. Kathleen went twice to her father's bedside. The first time was before the injection had been given. He was quite conscious and was able to speak to her. He knew the truth then. Whether it had suddenly burst upon him or had been long realized subconsciously no one can say. If Dixon was telling nothing but the truth Fullam had known it for some time, and had accepted the inevitable with that fatalism which is so prevalent both in India generally and in this tragic tale. Kathleen broke down in court, and her eyes filled with tears each time she told the story.

> Father said: "I am going, Kathleen, dear. Be a good girl, and God will bless you. Give my love to Leonard, and tell him not to fret."
>
> He then asked: "Where's mother?"
>
> I replied: "In the dining-room. Shall I go and call her?"
>
> Father said: "No, dear. I do not want her."

He must have known. Kathleen mentioned at the trial that her mother showed no sign of grief except at the funeral, when she wept. This little bit of unconscious satire from an observant and exceptionally intelligent little girl of ten, fits in so well with all we know, that it must be true.

Meanwhile Clark had gone off on his bicycle, overtaken the bearer, and cycled on to the club, where he found Captain Dunne. He brought him to the house. Captain Dunne looked at the body, spoke to Mrs Fullam saying, "I am very sorry; I can do nothing; it is too late," which she knew as well as he did, and after staying about five minutes, departed. Next day he countersigned the death certificate given by Clark. At 5 p.m. on that day, the normal interval in India, Fullam was laid in his last resting place, where his body was to lie undisturbed no more than fourteen months. The funeral once over, the danger of discovery was past, so long as no one asked Kathleen questions, and no one happened to see one of Mrs Fullam's letters. In Meerut there were whisperings and rumours, uttered with bated breath. In Agra there was mere indifference. Agra was in complete ignorance except for three people. One was a woman, who, if she despised her husband, kept silence for the sake of the children whom she loved. The second was Joseph. The third was the child Kathleen, who was forbidden by her mother to speak of her father's death because it was too sad. And the child obeyed her mother until the latter was arrested.

8
Calm

It is doubtful whether any murder by poisoning was ever carried out amongst Europeans or Anglo-Indians, particularly in official circles, so cleanly, if one may use the term, and so successfully, without exciting suspicion. How it happened that no suspicion was aroused amongst the doctors is a medical question, and is dealt with in the next chapter. Mrs Fullam at once settled down in Agra, with her children, to a normal existence as a widow receiving the attentions of an ardent lover. She seems to have lost none of her attraction for Clark, and she lavished upon him all the warmth of her ardent nature. He kept the compromising letters in a despatch box in her bungalow. Probably the true explanation of this strange conduct was that he felt that so long as he had them he possessed a complete hold over her until he had succeeded in getting rid of his wife. But it seems incredible that she should have permitted it. It was like sitting on a volcano. She may have thought that in her own house they were safe from discovery, though Mrs Clark knew of the existence of the box and its contents. Mrs Fullam had only one other thing to fear, and that was Kathleen. She successfully silenced her by the bold but motherly method of forbidding her to mention her father's death, warning her that if she did so she would bring trouble on those she loved. This could not have referred to Clark. Although he had been discreetly kind and attentive to the children in Meerut, he became harsh towards them in Agra because the poor little things wished to be with their mother, and he found them in the way. "He wanted her all to himself, so he beat us well," was the quaint summary of the situation given at the trial by the ten-year-old Kathleen.

Mrs Fullam was financially worse off than she had been, and eventually in July, 1912, she moved from Metcalfe Road, into a share of a bungalow in Cantonments, in Garden Road, very much nearer the Clarks. But she had money of her own, she was a clever manager, and she seems to have been peaceful and happy. She was not now above taking money and presents from Clark. But she had enough in the bank to be able to draw a cheque for Rs 100, to pay the hired assassins of Mrs Clark. Very few letters came to light, written during the year of calm, upon which she had now entered, and there is little to throw light upon her life. She must have often thanked God, in her curious way, for His manifold mercies vouchsafed unto her, and she certainly never betrayed the slightest pangs of conscience. This is clearly shown by such letters as we have.

Three days after the funeral she writes:

> I know you will love to receive these few lines from me this morning, because you count it a privilege, I am sure, to get my handwriting. Sweetheart mine, I felt so happy and blissful last night, when we parted, and you called me your "precious darling" and your "Heart's own Queen". Oh, darling, I retired to rest for the night so very happy and I thought to myself "my Harry loves me and cares for me with a deep, true, pure love, more than anyone else on earth has ever loved me." How good it is, my own darling, to be so dearly loved by a strong, tender man, it is "more precious than rubies." Harry darling, sweetheart mine, you know what a dreadful, anxious time I have gone through lately, in fact, we both have gone through. Is it any wonder then that I should look pale and washed out, my sweetie? You don't look pale or tired, but much happier and contented, and the very picture of strong, vigorous manhood, and just what a fine, muscular, sunburnt doctor should be, lovie Bucha. Now please don't you worry about giving me a tonic. I am all right and quite happy, darling, and you are my best and only tonic. I never dreamt that I could ever be so happy in this life, my Bucha darling, and I hope one day we shall both be happier even than we are now.
>
> Sweetheart darling, let me now take this opportunity of thanking you very heartily for all your kindness to me and

mine since coming to Agra. How very good and thoughtful you have been, my heart's treasure? Every little detail for our comfort has been planned and ordered by you, darling, and I have watched and noticed it all and loved you all the more.

On the 16th October she says:

Sweetheart, darling, I know that letter was written to me during the stress and strain of your morning's work, and I cannot thank you enough, my own Bucha darling, for all the trouble you take over me and all the goodness you show towards me. There is nothing too good for me in your eyes, lovie, neither is there any sacrifice too great for you to make. I only hope this devoted, passionate love of yours will last, my Bucha darling, even to the end of our lives on earth.

Sweetheart mine, what did Mrs C. have to say on your arrival home last night? Did she get very angry at your uniform being returned, darling? I am so sorry if you have got into any trouble and had her nagging tongue about your ears, my own lovie Bucha. Never mind, cheer up, my darling. With me it will be all so different; you will then know and realize what a true loving wife can make a home for a man.

She did not forget her old friends in Meerut:

Lovie, darling, to-day is just one year since we closed poor Mrs S.'s eyes. What a lot we have gone through together. God bless my lovie.

Towards the end of October the shadow of approaching separation again crossed her path and temporarily darkened her thoughts. Her own family, extending to her their sympathy in her bereavement, wanted her to return home, while Clark received warnings and rumours, so common with those in service in India, of the possibility of his transfer, either to Aden or to Delhi:

> Sweetheart mine, I have got an urgent call from my people to come home to them at once without delay. But how can I ever go far away and leave you, my ever dearest, darling Harry, to mope and fret and live a solitary, unhappy, wandering, restless life? My place is most certainly here, by your dearest side, ever ready to help, comfort and cheer you with my love and presence, darling. I have made my decision and will not leave you, until you yourself turn me away, or turn away from me. Then I shall leave Agra, never again to meet you, Bucha. May God grant that sad day may never come, dearie, although Miss Mugh (who told fortunes with cards, and whom Clark often consulted at Mrs Fullam's request) foretells it so plainly. But rather may we two most loving and devoted sweethearts be drawn together by love, closer and nearer, in the sweet ties and bonds of matrimony, which is the sweetest slavery on God's earth.
>
> Those who profess much practise little, and those who practise always, profess not at all; thus strong love, like smooth water, runs deep with constancy and an abiding attachment making no show on the surface, by lying ever tranquilly at the bottom.

~

My ever dearest, very own precious Harry sweetheart, Bucha darling—

Many, many thanks for your most loving, devoted and always welcome letter handed to me by dearest self yesterday, and which I appreciate most thoroughly, my own darling. Bucha lovie, we were both made most sad and unhappy all day yesterday by the foolish, light, frivolous talk of other people's tongues, darling. But what I only hope and pray will never come to pass at present, is your transfer to a distant station. Lovie darling, when I think how Miss M. prophesied a transfer for you soon, and to an unhealthy place, too, then I begin to wonder if the change to Aden will take place, darling. For Aden is a most unhealthy place, full of fevers. Oh, darling, our love will surely stand the test of waiting and separation even, if it so pleases the Almighty, who knows the depth of our love for each other. If you go away to Aden, then I only hope things will happen so that I may be able to accompany you, darling. I feel too much upset and sad to write more to-day, lovie Bucha.

Gussie

Till death, my own precious darling, for nothing but
death shall divide us, my sweet.

But the shadows soon passed. On the 13th of November she writes:

"'Tis well to be merry and wise,

   'Tis well to be honest and true,

   'Tis well to be off with an old love,

Before you get on with the new."

Love is a tender herb, which must be kept alive by great delicacy, it must be fenced from all inclement blasts, or it will droop its head and die.

A woman who truly loves asks but one question, whether he whom she loves gives her his heart in earnest, my own darling.

Sweetheart mine, how things seem to be working together, in bringing us two lovers nearer and dearer together. You are not going to Delhi after all, and no signs of a transfer yet. I only hope we can go together, darling, when it really comes.

She had adopted a new style. Her letters are as gushing as ever, but she was evidently reading a great deal and leading a peaceful and contented existence, and she takes to heading her letters with quotations. They all followed the same line of thought, but she made her selections with some taste and discrimination. So she writes shortly afterwards:

As the atmosphere invisibly surrounds the earth, yet is felt by all, so love unseen, pervades every breast, though its temperature varies according to the heart that gives it birth.

When a man has made up his mind to seek a wife, neither the influence of others, nor surroundings, can deter him from the point, much less the possibility of non-acceptance. He will stake all or lose all, my very own precious darling.

My ever dearest, very own precious Harry sweetheart, Bucha darling—

Good morning, my lovie; how are you this bright, beautiful, sunlit day? I am well and blooming, I am glad to say, and my heart is light, because my baby Myrtle is so much better. Oh, how clever and good and kind you are, Harry darling, to ease her so quick, break her fever, and put my most anxious mind at rest, darling. Sweetheart mine, Miss W. must have received your black-edged letter this morning. I wonder how she will answer it, my darling. I naturally feel very anxious over your old love and her correspondence, because I am sure she will never let you alone; her death-card was but a blind to renew your writing.

Well, let's see how things go? I am sure you would not care to be in my shoes, would you, darling? Sweetheart mine,

I love you so passionately and devotedly, that I hate anyone else to step between us, darling, or draw your thoughts away from me at all.

A day or two later she writes again in a similar strain, and gives an interesting insight into her constant passion for letter-writing. The reference to "Mrs Clarkson" is, of course, to the name in which Clark used to address her letters to the Post Office in Meerut. The complaint about the delay in receiving her pay will meet with a responsive echo in the heart of every reader who has been in service in India, and who has had to claim either back-pay, pension, or special allowances:

I am only too pleased to lift my pen and give you a few sweet loving lines to-day, if in so doing, you will find any pleasure, lovie. My own darling, why do you so love to get my letters? Do they remind you of those happy days when Mrs Clarkson was alive? Poor thing! She passed away very peacefully, and you have found a more lovable Buchee. Love, when mutual, gives and expects nothing less than the entire soul of man and woman, and enforces as an absolute duty that truth of which marriage is but the outward sign, seal, and ratification, viz., "What God hath joined together, let no man put asunder." Letters mean nothing, except that they are sometimes a natural relief to the heart, and the effort of pleasing a friend gives the writer good spirits in spite of himself. My own darling, I know you will say, "You are a very mischievous little girlie," but darling, you have a little gem in me, and the best girl in the whole world, so not, another word, sir.

Harry, sweetheart, my very own precious lovie, darling pet, my troubles are not over yet, regarding the Depy.

Comp., and the ten days' pay, but I will soon settle them, and knock the money out of the office. You must help me, Bucha darling, to go before the Civil Judge. There is nothing you would not help me in, I know, and you really spoil me by giving me always the very best of everything, lovie.

Her possession already of Clark's despatch-box, containing these letters, carefully endorsed and tied away in bundles, is shown by her letter of the 30th of November, the last of the series containing anything of substance throwing light upon the story. She has been going through her letters, and destroying some. Why she thought it "best" to destroy about a dozen and to leave about four hundred, is one of the puzzles presented by her baffling character, with its wonderful blend of intelligence and folly, of cold-blooded villainy and warm affection, of dastardly criminality, and deep religious fervour. "It is very interesting," she says, "to read some of my letters." She is right. And as she does so she falls to brooding over the past once more, and all that she has gone through. She seems to have no sense of shame; yet she was a proud woman. She seems to have no thought for her orphaned children, and yet she was very fond of them. And while still contemplating a fresh murder, she bursts into a cry of gratitude for all that the Almighty has done, as she persuades herself so easily, for her selfish little soul, and for the despicable man she loves:

I am beginning your usual letter rather later than I do daily, because I have been very busy sorting out some of my letters from your box, darling, and have burnt about a dozen or so, I didn't count them. It's best to do this, Harry Bucha, my own lovie darling pet, sweetheart mine. I will walk over to see you again this evening, and hope I will be in no one's way, sweetie. Look not mournfully to the past; it cometh not back again—wisely improve the present, it is thine.

Patience and perseverance overcome all difficulties, my very own darling. The great remedy which Heaven has put in our hands is patience by which, though we cannot lessen the torments of the body, we can in a great measure preserve the peace of the mind. So let us be patient and also brave, lovie Bucha, Harry darling, it is very interesting to read some of my letters of the past. How God has worked out all things so beautifully and brought us two most devoted and loving sweethearts close together, and given us freely to each other, here in Agra.

The happy climax is still to come, darling, and let us hope and pray it will not be very far away, but will terminate in our happy union and long married life, always together, my beloved.

I am quite sure we shall be very happy in our wedded life, my darling, for ours is a true love match, isn't it?

Meanwhile, Clark was renewing the attempts which he made from time to time to poison his wife. We have already seen the effort he had made in April 1911, and how it was frustrated by the servant, Bibu, whom he employed to do it. We have seen also how well aware Mrs Clark was of the attempts he was making. Mrs Fullam said that Clark had told her that he had tried to poison her long ago when he was stationed in Calcutta. She also admitted knowledge of the attempts he made during the time that she herself was living in Agra. Clark seldom or never dined with his family. He took his dinner at Mrs Fullam's and used to return home, when he had nothing else to do, at about 10 p.m. Mrs Clark was not likely to allow him to have anything to do with her food, and having failed in his efforts with the conscience-smitten Bibu, he employed a miserable creature called Buddhu, who turned informer, and at the trial gave evidence of the murder of Mrs Clark in November, in which he had taken a leading part. This man was really a hospital servant, and Clark had brought him from the hospital to be the table servant at the house, and to work the two services together. At the same time Mrs Clark, who was no doubt satisfied that he would also be pressed into the service of compassing her death by poison, used to give him extra pay of six rupees per month, out of her own pocket. So Buddhu did fairly well, and served at least two masters. He was made of that useful material from which informers are extracted. Operations were opened upon him by Mrs Fullam herself, who came to the bungalow one day and, according to Buddhu, offered him fifty rupees if he would give Mrs Clark something to eat, explaining that Clark was a doctor, and that it would do her good. But this was not good enough for Buddhu. Then Clark had a turn, and used threats, holding over the head of the unfortunate man the risk of the loss of his job at the hospital. This worked better, for Buddhu took three powders from Clark, with instructions to put them in Mrs Clark's tea. But the "Memsahib" generally made her own tea, so Buddhu plaintively reported to his master, and the plot hung fire. The day came when Mrs Clark was not well, and asked Buddhu to make her Chota hazri (early morning tea). He did, and Mrs Clark was violently sick. This was always her salvation, and explains why Clark referred to her in conversation with Mrs Fullam and Mr Alick Joseph as "poison proof". Mrs Clark did nothing except to complain to Buddhu about the tea, and to remark quietly to her daughter Louisa that her father was trying to poison her. Clark finally abandoned this line of attack, not without punishing the unfortunate servant, whom he dismissed from his employment at the hospital. Buddhu was very unhappy, even with his extra and secret remuneration of six rupees from Mrs Clark, and he said in his evidence that he did what is a favourite dodge with Indian servants, who seldom possess moral courage—he did his work badly in order to annoy Mrs Clark, and to induce her to get rid of him. But he did not want to lose his place at the hospital, and Mrs Clark did not want to lose so clumsy a poisoner, whose efforts to commit crime were no better than the normal work for which he held himself out to the world. So after many alarums and excursions, and petitions to the P.M.O., Buddhu was reinstated at the hospital, and continued also to work as table servant to Mrs Clark. In this capacity, during the hot weather of 1912, he received from Clark a bottle containing some liquid, with instructions to put it in Mrs Clark's food. This the ungrateful man actually did. But with a certain low cunning, he put very little, again serving two masters, which was one of his most pleasing weaknesses. Whether this bottle contained a mild dose of "heatstroke" mixture, or what other concoction the evil genius of Clark selected on this occasion, does not appear. The stuff was put into some rice, or pilau, which the family were taking as their first course at dinner. Mr White, another Assistant-Surgeon at the hospital, under Clark, was dining with the Clarks, but Clark himself was not there. Mrs Clark "had hopes" of

White for Louisa. The effect of the pilau upon Mrs Clark was immediate, and her symptoms were not unlike those of the wretched Mr Fullam. She got up from the table, went into her room, vomited, and lay down. She was attended by Mr White, who saw nothing to arouse suspicion. She was not likely to enlighten him.

Mrs Clark was devoted to her children, and went over to stay at Meerut with her son Harry as often as she could. She contemplated leaving Agra for good and living with her sons. Why she did not do so promptly, and leave Clark to his fate, the reader must decide for himself. She could have obtained a divorce from the court of the District Judge in Agra, rapidly and cheaply. Clark was not likely to defend a suit. Had she done this, or even quietly left her husband without taking proceedings, she would have saved her own life and that of her husband, while the cause of Mr Fullam's death would have remained a secret known only to his wife and Clark. She went to Meerut in August, and it was there that she wrote one of the most interesting private documents ever published written by a woman about her unhappy home life, in the form of a soliloquy. It was found locked away in her room after her death. It was evidently intended for one of her sisters in Calcutta. It may have been sent, and the paper found may have been a copy kept by her. It is a pathetic document, and one's heart bleeds for the unfortunate woman as one peruses it. It does her infinite credit, but it leaves one with a feeling of wonder and bewilderment, that any woman capable of putting that much on paper, even for a sister's eyes, should be content to let it rest there. The reader must draw his own conclusions as to what was her real intention and state of mind. Only such extracts from it are given here, as bear upon the double crime with which we are concerned. Passing from it for a moment, it is only necessary further to relate that, after returning to Agra, when her visit of August was over, she and her daughter Louisa paid another visit to her sons at Meerut in November. She was then in the best of health, and in her normal spirits. While she was away Clark and Mrs Fullam, convinced that more subtle means were unavailing, with the assistance of the ever-ready assassin, Buddhu, hatched the plot for her death by violence. "Let us hope that when she returns, darling," wrote Mrs Fullam to Clark, "our dearest hopes will be realized. Oh, how happy I should be!" Mrs Clark returned to Agra on the 14th of November, and was murdered by a hired gang on the night of the 17th. The following are the extracts from her soliloquy, about her life, written in August:

Meerut. 16th August, 1912, Friday.

No. 1—Why is Mr Clark always angry with me and my three children.

No. 2—Mr Fullam died in Agra on the 10th of October, 1911, in No. 9 Metcalfe Street, Agra.

No. 3—Mrs Fullam has been living in Agra ever since her husband's death.

No. 4—All my friends in Agra tell me that Mrs Fullam is living with my husband as his wife for the last year when Mr Fullam was alive in Meerut.

No. 5—Mr Clark has got an increase of pay, from March 1912, and he got a lot of back pay, but he only gave me a hundred, and I don't know what he has done with the rest of the money.

No. 6—From the last four months Mr Clark gives me two hundred and fifty rupees, and keeps fifty rupees and sixty rupees sub-charge.

No. 7—I have been told that Mr Clark has kept Mrs Fullam as his wife and allows her fifty rupees a month, and that she is going to get a baby very soon, and when I die he is going to marry her.

No. 8—Ever since I have left Calcutta to come to Agra we have been transferred to many stations; first of all we came to Agra Fort, and when we were there we were all very ill, and I nearly died over there as my cook poisoned me; must be through Mr Clark's help.

No. 9—We only stayed there a year, when we were transferred to Chakrata Hills, and we stayed there only a year, and during that time I was very ill and nearly died, as Gopi, the ward servant's wife, did witchcraft me very badly, that I broke out in sores all over my body.

No. 10—We came to Meerut, and stayed there two years, or a few months more. There even I was very ill with a bad sore on my left cheek, that the Medical Officer had to come and see me twice a day. It was in this station that Mr Clark got to know Mr and Mrs Fullam.

No. 11—We were sent to Delhi Fort, and we did not stay there long, as Mr Clark was only going on leave to Meerut to see Mrs Fullam, and the Medical Officer did not like him doing so; then he was sent to Agra, and we are there ever since; and would like to know very much how long we are going to stay in Agra, and to what other station we will have to go, as Mr Clark has become very wicked ever since we have gone to Agra, as he keeps very bad company.

No. 12—When first we came to Agra from Delhi I brought a very good cook with me, but he ran away back to Delhi very soon after as he told me that Mr Clark gave him three white powders to give me in the tea, and if he did not do so that Mr Clark would kill him, but he ran away and gave back the dry poison to my son, Harry.

No. 13—Last month I was very ill, vomiting, as my cook gave me something in my tea. I dismissed him without giving him his pay.

No. 14—Last month I was very ill with vomiting all night the day of the Sitla Mela, and if it was not for two assistant surgeons by the name of Jacob and White, I am sure I would have died that very night.

No. 15—On the 11th of August my son Harry came to Agra and brought my son Walter and my daughter Maud and myself away with him to Meerut, and he arrived in Meerut on the morning of the 13th, and we are feeling ever so much better over here....

No. 18—I am perfectly sick and tired living with Mr Clark, and would like to live for good with my son Harry, as I fear he will be putting up the new servant to poison our food as soon as we go back to Agra....

No. 24—Mr Clark and his brother are selling their grandfather's house for six thousand rupees, and both the brothers will get three thousand each. What will Mr Clark do with all his money? Give it away to Miss W., Mrs Fullam, or leave it to his three children? His gold watch, and the seal are all at Mrs Fullam's house, with a box full of letters from different women. Will Mrs Fullam go along with him to the next station, or will she remain back in Agra? Such a wicked woman should be put to death.

No. 25—After Walter gets work to do, and Maud gets married, won't it be better to separate from Mr Clark for good, and live with my son Harry, as I would be afraid to trust my life alone with him, as he is not a good man? I would be much happier away from him, and he could give me a good monthly allowance. I do not like him one bit now, since he has become so cruel to my dear children and myself. He does nothing towards making us happy, and never takes us out. The whole time he is in the company of wicked people, who are always seeking to do him harm. He may be going to the dogs if he is allowed to have his own way. Miss W—— still writes to him, as she has a good hold of him.

9

Storm

The murder of Mrs Clark in her bed on the night of Sunday, the 17th of November, from the point of view of a Superintendent of Police in India, compared to all that preceded and led up to it, was a simple and squalid affair. But it not unnaturally raised a storm of excitement in Agra. Clark was almost immediately suspected of having had a hand in it. The reason for this will become apparent the moment the details of the crime are examined. Murder in India is common enough, especially by violent means. There is probably not a bazaar of any size which does not contain scores of reckless ruffians, ready to sell their services, either to commit perjury, to invent a false alibi, or to rob, beat, or murder, for a few rupees. But except for cases of assassination for political motives, the murder of either a European or an Eurasian is rare, and the murder of an Eurasian woman, in an important and largely populated station like Agra, is almost unheard of. So that although the means adopted were simple and conventional, the purpose was something quite out of the common, and calculated to awaken not only excitement but curiosity. Clark's character and his relations with his unhappy wife were well known in Agra, and though no one would have expected him to break out into such a desperate act as murder by violence, the absence of any satisfactory explanation of an attack on the Clark bungalow, and upon Mrs Clark herself in particular, was certain to turn men's thoughts in the direction of her husband.

We have seen that Clark and Mrs Fullam were tired of waiting for the consummation of their hopes. Possibly the fact that Mrs Fullam was aware that she was likely to have a child in the course of the coming summer, although Clark was usually equal to doing what was necessary to prevent this calamity, may have accelerated their plans. Whether that had anything to do with it or not, they were losing patience, and were awaiting Mrs Clark's return from her visit to her son at Meerut. She arrived back home on the 14th of November. Buddhu, the "universal provider" of murder in all its forms at short notice, had left the service of the Clarks. He was free to do any sort of murderous work in the Clark establishment with less risk of suspicion attaching to him than had been formerly the case. So to Buddhu this repulsive pair turned in their need, and he was easily induced by the promise of what would seem to him comparative wealth, to find some congenial ruffians amongst his friends and associates. It did not take him long. On the 14th of November Mrs Fullam drew a cheque for one hundred rupees from her account at the Bank of Bengal, and on the same day Clark endorsed and cashed it for ten notes of ten rupees each. This was imprudent, but Clark was always full of confidence and optimism, but both of them in this their last venture displayed some overconfidence. One hundred rupees was the contract price, according to the subsequent confession of Buddhu. He added that it was not enough, and that they all said so. This statement raises some nice questions, but it is certain that this inadequate sum was more than they got! No one at the trial asked Buddhu what he or anyone else considered sufficient. It would not be an easy question to answer, except by the obvious reply that the true price is what you can get. On this question of barter and the "higgling of the market", there are certain to be difficulties. It must be annoying for the contractor to part with his money in advance, and to see his hirelings decamp with the cash without performing their part of the bargain. This was not the sort of mistake which Clark was likely to make. On the other hand it is equally distressing to the hirelings to receive nothing but encouragement and promises, and to have to make off to another place of residence in order to escape the attentions of the police without any reward for their trouble. Little Kathleen threw some light on what happened in this connection. On Sunday evening, when Mrs Fullam's servants were out, she saw two men, Buddhu and a friend, arrive at her mother's place and enter the pantry. There a long conversation took place between them and Mrs Fullam and Clark, and a great part of it was taken up by the subject of money. On the morning of Tuesday, the 19th, one of them, Sukkha, the darzi, returned, and would not be satisfied until Mrs Fullam had gone into the house and brought him some cash, in which notes were included. It would have been like Clark to have drawn the money from Mrs Fullam's bank, and to have left her to pay the demands of the murderers. The shrewdness and the presence of mind of Kathleen are demonstrated by the circumstance that she remarked to Sukkha that he was not really a darzi, and that she might tell. There can be little doubt that she had always suspected that her father had been murdered by her mother, and that she believed that the violent death of Mrs Clark had been brought about by these low-caste young men who were haunting her mother's bungalow and demanding money. The final arrangements had been made at Mrs Fullam's on the Sunday evening. The names of these heroes, who were all young men, but full adults, according to Indian ideas, were Buddhu, chamar, 23; Buddha, banjar, 23; Sukkha, darzi, 20; Mohan, 20, known as "percher, and City Man", who had the sword with which they smashed Mrs Clark's head; and one, Ram Lal, kachi, 22, who was eventually acquitted on the strength of an alibi.

Clark gave them to understand that they would find the front door of the verandah open. In this they were disappointed. Clark had industriously put it about that he had just drawn his salary, and he had mentioned to his daughter that the money should be carefully put away because there were thieves about. So the murderers found the doors closed. It was not difficult to withdraw the bolt of one, because the pane of glass on one of its panels was broken, so that one could put his arm in, but Clark had reckoned without the bull terrier—a strange oversight—and the dog barked, so the men withdrew into the compound. Meanwhile, Clark, in order to provide himself, not merely with an alibi, but with a motive for his absence from home in the middle of the night, while desiring to keep in close touch with it, went off to the railway station on the pretence of meeting a friend. He stayed there for an hour in conversation with the Assistant Station Master, and waited till the Mail arrived at 12.45. He then returned home hoping to find his wife dead. He found, however, all quiet, and the murderers still waiting in the compound. They could tackle a woman in her sleep but a dog was too much for them, even though they had a sword. Clark let himself in, removed the sheet from his bed in order, apparently, to stifle the dog, and shut up the dog in an outhouse. At about half-past one the attack was delivered. Miss Clark was sleeping in the same room, and tried to intervene, but was threatened by one of the men with a big stick. She was, of course, powerless, and after fracturing Mrs Clark's skull by two blows from the sword and inflicting some minor cuts upon her, the men fled. They did not touch Miss Clark, and though they rummaged some drawers, they stole practically nothing. Clark arrived shortly afterwards, and was greeted by his daughter with the terrible news. The gap between Clark's departure from the railway station and his arrival at home, was a clue for the police. He did not lose much time in summoning Walker and White, his fellow medical officers, and he then went off to Mrs Fullam, who advised him to go to his Commanding Officer, Major Buchanan. It was three o'clock when he got there, and it was three-fifteen when he and Major Buchanan arrived at the Cantonment Police Station. The latter said that he noticed that it had not occurred to Clark to go there, and that it was at his own suggestion that they went straight off together. Clark made a statement which was taken down in writing by Inspector Smith at ten o'clock. He said that he had been at the station to meet a man named Joikim, who was travelling through from Delhi to Bombay. This was a terrible mistake, and was immediately noticed by the Inspector, because Agra is not on the route. When he had finished the statement he corrected the name, and said it was a man named Menzies, the champion draughts player, whom he was going to meet. This was worse, for not only did it seem impossible that he could have made a mistake about a friend whom he was going to meet at the train less than twelve hours before, but he had given the name of Joikim to Mrs Fullam. When Inspector Smith took Mrs Fullam's statement in the afternoon she was induced to say that Clark had told her he was going to meet Joikim. The police had now a good deal to go upon. The relations between Clark and his wife were notoriously bad. Mrs Fullam told the police that they were good. The dog had failed to bark, and had been missing when Miss Clark was awakened. The removal of Clark's bedsheet was mysterious. Moreover, nothing of any value had been taken by the murderers, and it was clear that it was not an ordinary robbery with murder. What motive had four men for such a useless and barbarous crime upon a defenceless woman in her sleep? Why had they murdered the mother and not touched the daughter? Mrs Clark could only mutter a few words, and she died about mid-day from a fractured skull. Clark was arrested in the afternoon of the 18th November.

The Superintendent of the Police took the matter in hand from the first and showed great decision. On the 19th he sent Inspector Smith to search Mrs Fullam's bungalow. There was not the slightest reason for supposing that she was in the conspiracy, but her relations with Clark were known, and Clark told the police that he had dined with her on the evening of the crime. The search was undertaken with the hope that something belonging to Clark might be found there. The hope was justified by the finding of several things, but Nemesis, or the God in whom Mrs Fullam trusted, had delivered the criminals into the hands of Justice by an accident almost without parallel. As he was leaving, Inspector Smith struck his foot against a tin box underneath Mrs Fullam's bed. He asked what it was. Mrs Fullam said that it was Lieutenant Clark's despatch box. She no doubt felt a little pride in the possession of a military accessory of such high-sounding importance. Inspector Smith asked for the key, and Mrs Fullam told him that it was with Clark. She said she would get it and give it him to-morrow. But Inspector Smith wanted the box. He broke it open, and there were the packets of letters, which Mrs Fullam had written to Clark, and which she had told him "it is best to destroy". Mrs Fullam said nothing to the inspector, but turned a bright scarlet.

Inspector Smith put his own padlock on the box, and took it away. Shortly afterwards Mrs Fullam was arrested, and on 6th December her husband's body was exhumed.

III

THE MEDICAL ASPECT

1

It has already been observed that the Agra poisoning case presents one feature which has no parallel in the history of medical jurisprudence. The reader will remember that in the month of April 1911, when Clark and Mrs Fullam first conspired to poison Fullam, Clark had been transferred to the hospital at Agra, while the Fullams were still living at Meerut. The poison was supplied by Clark to Mrs Fullam through the post, and administered to Fullam by his wife, who, as we have seen, kept up an almost daily correspondence with her lover. As a natural consequence of this, those who are interested in the medical aspect of this remarkable story have the advantage of a continuous record in writing, contemporaneous with the administration of the deadly doses, of the symptoms manifested by the victim.

In the first stage of the conspiracy, arsenic was undoubtedly the agent selected. It has always been the prime favourite of the poisoner in India, and the reasons for this preference are not far to seek. It is almost tasteless, and is easily procurable in any bazaar. In those days, even if any attempt has been made to remedy the defect to-day, there was no law either compelling the vendor to record the transaction, or requiring the purchaser to sign any document recording his purchase, or to disclose his identity. In a country like India, where the vast majority of the population are illiterate; where some shops in the bazaar are of mushroom growth, and dealers are here to-day and gone to-morrow, while the majority are more concerned to defeat regulations, than, to obey them; any legislation of the kind with which we are familiar in England, would be only a dead letter.

Apart altogether from its medicinal value, the legitimate uses of arsenic in India are numerous. It is much employed as a preservative agent, especially for wood, and in preparing hides and skins. It is also constantly used for the destruction of vermin. In a tropical country, moreover, its poisonous effects are so frequently simulated by natural disease that suspicion is far less likely to be aroused than in healthier climates. Cholera, diarrhoea, gastro-enteritis, and irregularities of the stomach and bowels generally, are regarded as the common lot of humanity, and the symptoms of these diseases closely resemble those of arsenical poisoning, either acute or chronic. The Hindu custom of burning the dead has saved many a poisoner from the discovery of his crime. Once the victim is dead, the body burned, and the ashes consigned to the Sacred River, there may be suspicion, but there can be no proof.

Clark, as we know, was born and bred in India. He had lived all his life in an Indian atmosphere, and must have been familiar with these facts. Eastern ideas and Eastern thought play a large part in the "make-up" of such a man. It is even possible that he inherited from his Hindu ancestry the belief, curious to occidental notions, that murder by poisoning is a less heinous crime than murder by the shedding of blood. Be that as it may, he not unnaturally turned first to arsenic. We have already seen that he had more than once attempted to poison his wife by the same means, and had complained to his friend Joseph—"the Agra letter-writer"—that she was "poison proof". To find a parallel for the astounding naiveté of this complaint one must surely go back to the days of Benevenuto Cellini! In the case of Fullam, Clark's tentative use of the poison was remarkable. It is more than likely that his medical knowledge of the drug was deficient, and that he was unaware that moderate doses can be tolerated for some time without serious effects, and even with actual benefit. If his medical knowledge was adequate, we must fall back on the conclusion that he had a difficult course to steer between the Scylla of large doses, with probable discovery, and the Charybdis of small doses and futility. On the 17th of June, however, it is clear that he caused Mrs Fullam to administer something like a lethal dose, but this was after two months of experiment. The symptoms of the victim during these two months are detailed by Mrs Fullam in her letters to Clark, and make a record which is unique, and, in any case, worthy of close study. On the 20th of April Clark visited Mrs Fullam in Meerut and left with her a number of "tonic powders". The first mention of the administration of these is to be found in a letter written shortly after this date:

> You are anxious to know about the "tonic". Well, sweetheart darling, I have given it regularly since I last saw you, and I must say it is a good tonic, in very truth, darling. My hubby is quite well and strong, and it really seems to have done him good. I shall certainly continue it, lovie, and let you know later. How is Mrs Clark, your lawful wife?

The polite inquiry after the health of Mrs Clark is due to the fact that at this time she was undergoing the same arsenical treatment as Mr Fullam. On the 26th of April Mrs Fullam writes that the effects are still unsatisfactory, and that the arsenic is beginning to exert its well-known aphrodisiac effects:

> Sweetheart mine, my hubby seems quite unaffected by the tonic powders. In fact, he is stronger and better than before, and more passionate, if such can be the case, in his case, my own darling. Some days I give him two, or even three powders, my Bucha dearest, but never less than one. I want you to let me know in return what you think of it, my own precious sweetie, and tell me how to go on?

Next day some irritant effect on the stomach and bowels is being produced, but Mrs Fullam deplores its transitory action:

> Now, darling, you are very thoughtful in sending me some more powders. I was going to ask you for some, as I have only two left. Yesterday I gave my hubby three during the day, and he came back from the office at 6 p.m. with pains in his stomach, had a loose motion, and felt weak. He soon pulled up, however, and now seems quite well, darling. I don't think these powders are having any effect, Bucha. What do you

think, lovie? You say they must be given regularly, and then you say you can't administer them to Mrs C. as regularly as you would like to. Then what is the use of them, darling? She will need much more than that, lovie. However, tell me plainly what you think.

On the 4th of May, after receiving a further stock of powders from Clark, in which he had evidently increased the dose, she again complains of the aphrodisiac effect of the doses:

You will undoubtedly be glad to hear that I screwed up my courage to give one powder yesterday, Harry darling, but no effect so far, except as a very good tonic. I make my husband very amorous, Bucha darling, and I don't want this, please. To-day another one will be administered, my sweetheart darling, and you will know results.

In a letter of this date the following passage occurs. Although the drug has been administered continuously for about a fortnight there have been no bad symptoms, except the constant stomach trouble, and Mrs Fullam's impatience is getting very pronounced:

Harry sweetheart, my hubby since yesterday has had slight stomach trouble, and nausea, which he attributes to an attack of indigestion, to which he is subject, darling. The powders are going on being administered steadily, darling, but there is little or no difference, except that my hubby feels the heat very much, and complains of being tired. But that's an old story. I wish to know, darling please, in reply to this, how long I am to continue this treatment, and when should desired results appear, Bucha?

On the 8th of May she again complains of the ineffectual powders:

> Now about the powders, Harry darling, I gave two on Saturday, in two cups of tea, you know, as I send his tiffin. But on Sundays only I never get a chance, Bucha. How many hundreds of years will they take? I must say I don't approve of your powders at all, darling.

On the 9th of May she again alludes to the tonic effects, and also draws his attention to the good effect of the drug upon the skin. It would seem, from a reference to a five-grain dose, that some sugar, or other harmless constituent was being mixed with the arsenic, as it is scarcely conceivable that such strong doses of pure arsenic could have been tolerated, and Clark had evidently not made up his mind, at this stage, to make the irrevocable plunge, by the swift administration of fatal doses. If he had, there is every reason to think that Fullam's condition was such, that he could have been despatched with small expenditure of time and trouble:

> Of course, I have not yet received the tonic powders you mention having sent, lovie, as I did not know anything about them until I read your letter, so I did not inquire about the tiny parcel at the P.O., but I suppose I shall get it to-morrow, and will let you know, Harry darling, sweetheart mine. My hubby is improving greatly on two of the old powders daily (you remember five grains each). His complexion has changed to a lovely pink. I have never seen him look better.

On the 20th of May, after a visit of Clark's to Meerut, a further unsuccessful administration of a new powder is referred to:

Yesterday I administered the powder you left with me, viz., the half-dose, my very own precious darling Bucha, with the result, nil. Not so much as the change of a hair's breadth, Harry darling, so I intend to let to-day and Sunday go by with no further administration. But I shall begin in earnest on Monday, and shall keep you informed of results.

Poor Fullam! "Black Monday", when he returned each week to the scene of his official labours, was beginning to have a new meaning for him. On the 23rd of May reference is made by Mrs Fullam for the first time to a new drug, jalapin, which is being administered, probably in combination with the arsenic. The reason for this is not obvious, and it gave rise to some suspicion, even in the mind of the long-suffering, but unsuspecting, Fullam:

Harry darling, my own precious Bucha, I have news for you, and you must tell me how to act. I administered the full dose in tea yesterday, but my hubby returned the whole jug of tea, untasted, from the office, saying it was bad. When he came home at six, I asked, him why he had returned his tea, and he said, "There was some bad medicine in it," so Harry darling, I dare not continue with these powders. He also said, "This is the second time the tea has tasted bad," which shows that the jalapin is readily tasted.

My Bucha darling, Fate is against us, and all our plans are utterly frustrated and have failed. What is to be done, darling? I feel so very disappointed and down-hearted, not so much on my own account as on account of you, for I know darling you want me so much, and the best prime years of your life are being wasted, without love, care, and comfort, darling. Now I want you to let me know two things in your reply, please, Harry Bucha. Tell me what to do with the powders I have by me, as I cannot give any more, for he can taste them, darling. (2) What is your opinion or best plan of operation for the future, my darling? It is an old saying, "Love will ever find a way", or "Where there's a will there's a way", Harry darling, so let me know exactly what you think. The first powders were tasteless and unsuspected, but not strong enough, but these jalapin ones do not suit at all, darling.

The letter of which the foregoing is an extract is doubly interesting. One cannot refrain from wondering how it was that Fullam himself, once his suspicions were aroused, and were connected in his mind, as they must have been, with what he had seen of his wife's friendship with Clark, and with the feeling of jealousy with which he was assailed from time to time, did not take a firmer line about the preparation and supply of his food. He had implicit confidence in his wife. But it was being badly shaken, and the truth really is that he possessed in his composition, much of the fatalism of the East. The other feature, which is brought out by this letter, is the tremendous confidence which Mrs Fullam had in herself, her personal attractions, and her irresistible fascination for Clark, which enabled her to persuade herself most completely that her love for him was wholly unselfish, and that she was necessary to his existence. It appears that Clark had, by the 26th of May, suggested that a dose of croton oil should be given "by mistake" for castor oil. Mrs Fullam, with her usual clear-sightedness, and logic, points out the difficulty about this, and asks Clark to decide upon the next step:

> Sweetheart, darling, I think your plan about the croton oil won't do, Bucha, because my hubby seldom or ever takes a dose of castor oil—he hates it. But I don't clearly understand you, my sweetie; you once say you are studying to take some other stuff, and then you say you can send me some more powders, if I let you know by return post. Darling sweet, have you decided on anything yet? And please do remember it must be tasteless, my Bucha. If my hubby were only in ill health, and I had to dose him at all, things would be very much easier, wouldn't they?

In his dislike to taking castor oil Mr Fullam was not singular, and he seems to have had sufficient authority in his own home to decline to be dictated to by his wife on the subject of aperients, which is more than can be said of everyone. There is an element of paradox about the situation as set forth in this letter, because, although the poor man must by this time have been almost saturated with arsenic, he was not seedy enough to please his wife, and Clark's efforts up to this stage have done no more than strengthen Fullam's defence against the further attacks which were in contemplation. None the less, on the 15th of June Mrs Fullam mentions for the first time another symptom of chronic arsenical poisoning, which was beginning to manifest itself in her husband, and which subsequently became very troublesome. This was a redness and irritation in the eyes, due to the excretion of arsenic through the lachrymal apparatus. On the same day in June Clark paid one of his visits to Meerut, and no doubt had to listen to a good deal of criticism from his accomplice, upon the apparent failure of his expert efforts. At any rate, he evidently determined that drastic action of some kind was called for, and that the time had come when the risk of administering a fatal dose must be faced. On the night of the 16th of June Fullam, unaware of Clark's recent visit, became very ill indeed, and had it not been that, like Mrs Clark, he vomited so successfully, and thus threw off a large quantity of the poison, the dose must certainly have proved fatal. No reference is made in the correspondence to its amount, which must therefore be a matter of conjecture. But it must have been several grains, at least, and may have been very much more. The actual story is best told in the following extracts from Mrs Fullam's letters of the 17th of June, and following days:

> Since four p.m.
> Vomited eight times, purged once.
> Vomited ten times at a quarter to nine.
> Vomited twelve times at ten p.m.
> Slept after that.

> June 17th
>
> Harry Darling,
>
> My hubby has been very ill all Friday night, since four o'clock, with symptoms of cholera. I got the Staff-Surgeon, Captain P——, to whom he is entitled, to treat him, and also Captain W—— has been kindly giving him help. I have been up all night giving him ice, &c. My hubby declares his last mouthful of tea and tiffin caused a burning sensation, and he started retching in office. My darling, I can't go to the P.O. this morning for your dearest letter, sweetheart, as I can't leave him, and I expect Capt. P—— any minute. They all blame the Masonic dinner on Thursday night, but he himself says the tiffin upset him, darling. You and I know

how. I cannot bear to see his suffering, Bucha darling. He has fever this morning, and is quite weak and prostrate, kept in bed, and on cornflour, cooked in water.

~

June 18th

He is very weak, Harry darling, and lies for hours with eyes closed, not speaking much or taking any notice of things. The retching has all stopped, but he complains of a soreness in his stomach, and seems weak, as I tell you. Also rush of blood to the head, and a headache.

~

June 21st

Oh! I have been through such an awful time lately! This week has seemed an eternity, and I have felt so lonely and miserable. My hubby is sick; he does not improve at all since that Friday night. He gets half a tonic powder every day, and his liver seems affected. He takes all sorts of medicine, Harry darling, and seems a different man. He now goes to office in the phaeton, and returns in it again for tiffin, after which he sleeps till five, and then goes for a drive. Sweetheart darling, I am acting on my own account entirely, as I have not received your letter, and do not know what directions you gave me, or anything. Anyhow, my own Bucha lovie, all for your sweet sake! I am not happy, as the whole tone and trend of this letter will show you, darling.

~

June 22nd

My hubby still continues ill. I have come here for a bottle of Sanatogen for him, dearie. (This must have been the

Post Office.) He has very bad dyspepsia, rush of blood to
the head, insomnia and all, and he is talking of going up to
Mussoorie on a few days' leave till the rains break.

An extract from a letter of the 24th of June shows that the medical officers who had seen Fullam during his attack, had not entertained any real suspicion of poisoning, though the idea had occurred to one of them. The reference to the Masonic banquet was not intended to throw any aspersions on the festive occasions indulged in by the craft, but merely voiced an idea prevalent in India, that public dinners are apt to be fraught with risk to the digestive organs, Mrs Fullam writes later as to this:

Sweetheart mine, as you wish to know, I must tell you that the Staff-Surgeon did not exactly state his diagnosis of my hubby's illness last Friday night; the only remark he made was, "Oh, Lord, you went to a Masonic Banquet last night," and then he laughed. But Capt. W——, the old duffer opposite, said the cause of such a severe illness was very strange, and when my hubby persistently told him of the scalding in his stomach as soon as he had swallowed the last mouthful of tea and tiffin, then he said, "If you had any enemies, I should say you were poisoned with arsenic poisoning." Harry darling, I firmly believe that my hubby suspects me because he said that the tiffin went to the office with some irritant poison in it. The whole thing has subsided and blown over now, Harry lovie, but you can imagine all I have gone through.

The old Captain was not such a duffer after all. He was quite right, and one of the most astounding features of this astounding story is that neither he, nor Fullam, followed it up, although the latter had formed, from time to time, quite definite suspicions, which would have led to his countering the attack which was being made upon his life, if he had only possessed the least force of character. For on the 16th of June the wife wrote:

> The powders I find very hard to administer, as he does not take any food prepared from my hand, makes his own cocoa, &c. Still I am doing my best.

This was certainly more than can be said of Fullam, who had only to wait for another administration, and to send a specimen to the "old duffer" for analysis. The eyes are still giving trouble on the 27th of June. Mrs Fullam, with a clinical acumen worthy of a better cause, comes to the undoubtedly correct conclusion that the "tonic powders" are to blame.

> Sweetheart mine, as my hubby has gone again to the Cantonment General Hospital to-day, to see Lieut. Monroe, I take the opportunity of writing my letter, Harry darling, not knowing what the day may bring forth, as his eyes are ordered complete rest, and he is going to apply for ten days' leave.... Now, Harry darling, please let me know by return post whether the tonic powder affects the eyes? I have an idea it does, lovie Bucha.

~

June 28th

I give half a tonic powder every day in his Sanatogen, lovie darling, because it lays on the top of the white powder (Sanatogen) quite unsuspiciously, and he mixes it up in his teaspoon. I find, by boiling into a solution as, you direct, Harry darling, the symptoms become much more severe as in Friday's case, darling, and there may be suspicion attached, having that scalding feeling down the throat. But this, in the Sanatogen, is a much easier way, don't you think, my Bucha darling? I told you I was doing my best, and you should trust me.

No poisoner ever worked harder, or with more varying success, under the directions of a supposed expert. Yet the sententious little criminal seems to blame herself with equal candour, whether she is meeting with success, or partial failure. But having been given leave on medical grounds, the unfortunate victim of the experiments made upon him by his wife and friend, obtained a respite from "tonic powders", and it is probable that the administration of arsenic ended with his departure for the Hills in July, though its effects continued for some time. On his return from the Hills, "his eyes are better, but still bloodshot." On the 18th of July his wife writes that, "his eyes are bloodshot, like a heavy drinker," though he was the most abstemious of men. On the 24th she says, "My hubby's eyes have been so bloodshot and bad that I have to read the newspapers to him. He has had to get the eyedrops that Col. M—— prescribed for him in Calcutta. His eyes are still red and raw looking." On the 26th of July, "His face is red, and his eyes bloodshot on account of the heat. He also seems to have a chronic cold and cough. Really, I have never seen a weaker, or more delicate man." The cold and cough were unquestionably due to the continued excretion of the arsenic through the respiratory passages. Later on she mentions "tingling in the feet and hands". Although this symptom came on after the administration of the "heatstroke mixture", it seems more likely that it was a slight peripheral neuritis, also due to the arsenic, than that it was caused by the atropine contained in the mixture.

So far, then, as arsenic was concerned, the chapter closed.* In spite of a continuous administration lasting over a period of about two-and-a-half months, with a larger dose on the 17th of June, the "consummation devoutly to be wished" by the conspirators seemed as far off as ever. Fullam's health was shattered, and his wife feared that he might become blind, but his death scarcely seemed a possibility. It was in these circumstances that a "brainwave" occurred to Mrs Fullam, which again narrowly missed complete success. Certain and infallible means of securing Fullam's speedy death, without risk of discovery, must have been the dominant motive of all future action, from this juncture. It is pointed out elsewhere in these pages that, having apparently discarded divorce, probably because it meant disgrace, whereas secret murder did not, they reached a stage when, if Fullam survived, he would have to retire, a helpless wreck, in pensioned penury, and all the hopes and schemes by which this criminal couple had been urged, and buoyed up, would be dashed to the ground.

---

* If any lingering doubt remained as to arsenic having been the chief agent employed up to this stage, it was set at rest when the body of Fullam was exhumed. The body was found, after more than a year in a cheap coffin in a tropical country, to be in a remarkable state of preservation, and arsenic was found in the thigh bone which was removed for analysis.

2

During Fullam's absence in the Hills, in the early part of July, the weather in Meerut became very hot and steamy, and several cases of heatstroke occurred. This suggested to the active brain of Mrs Fullam, the diabolically clever idea that a poison might be administered to her husband, the effects of which would simulate heatstroke. On the 11th of July the day before her husband returned, she writes:

> Harry, my own very precious sweetheart, I must mention to you that Mr N——, whom I think you know, got a heatstroke evening before last, and is seriously ill. He is about my hubby's height and build, with the same florid complexion. Do you think, lovie darling, that the same symptoms could be produced on someone we know? Especially now, coming down from the Hills to Meerut, which is at present very hot. More especially, darling, as he was suffering from cerebral congestion long before he went up. Let me know what you think of this, and if it can be done without suspicion whatever?

~

July 14th

> Can you forget all about me, and turn your thoughts away from your girlie, Gussie Buchee, or do you think we should try and use the means of the heatstroke, to be happy once again, darling love?... I have fully made up my mind about the heatstroke affair. Even if you never marry me, I can suffer! So please send me the powder one day next week, when convenient to you, darling, under a registered cover, and addressed to Mrs Clarkson, as usual, and please let me

know full instructions. Also how long after taking will the effect take place? He does not perspire so freely as you or I do, Bucha, but still there is slight moisture. His eyes are better, but still bloodshot.

Clark fell in with the heatstroke idea:

July 18th

Before you send me the liquid syrup containing the powder, write and let me know when to expect it. My hubby told me that one of the Hussar men had died of heatstroke that very afternoon. So I asked him what sort of death it was, and he said: "Oh, very easy; one of the easiest I know." So I warned him not to go working in the garden as he does, morning and evening, his face getting quite red. Really, Harry darling, I don't know how he escapes getting heatstroke. He gets amorous, but is weak. As you say, he is in a very favourable condition for it. His eyes are bloodshot still, as though he drank, and his face at times is almost purple. The only thing which keeps me back from doing it, my Bucha darling, is the thought of ways and means, and how to manage afterwards…I do not give any tonic powders, darling, as he does not need them, and I have no chance to administer them. The liquid will be quite enough.

~

July 19th

Thanks for letting me know in detail about the symptoms, darling. You know I have a very hard task before me. I am now anxious for your dear advice on all these matters, which torture my poor brain, day and night, darling. You can despatch the liquid by next Wednesday. I can call for the parcel personally, my own darling, as it will be risky sending it here.

On the 25th of July Mrs Fullam supplies interesting details of her proposed *modus operandi*, and fixes the date for the dose, which was actually adhered to, and the poison was administered according to plan:

> Sweetheart mine, I have fully made up my mind to try and administer the liquid on Thursday night, the 27th, at dinner, and I have ordered the cook to prepare mullighitawny soup, darling, so that we will eat it with rice, and add lime juice. So my own Bucha lovie, if you disguise the bitter taste with lime juice, or salt, darling, it will go well with the acid soup, and raise no suspicion, darling. Besides, on Thursday afternoon, I think we will be going to the Berkshire Sports, held in front of your old Section Hospital, Bucha lovie. So, as it is so hot and steamy, without a drop of rain, he will be supposed to have got a touch of the sun that afternoon, darling. So I think Thursday will be the best day to finish off this dreadful business. Don't you agree with me, my darling? I have no chance to put it in his lime juice and soda drinks, as he opens the bottle and pours it out himself, lovie. He and I both take Vermouth and lemonade at dinner, and if I had a chance I would mix it up in that, but he mixes it all up himself, so the only thing is the soup. I sincerely hope that no suspicion of any kind will attach itself to me or you, my own sweetie, and then after that, all will be plain sailing.

This is prophetic. No suspicion, worthy of the name, did arise, and all was "plain sailing", until, a year after Fullam's death, Inspector Smith's foot happened to strike against the tin box under the bed. On the 26th of July, Mrs Fullam asks for further advice about disguising the taste of the liquid with limes, &c. At the end of the letter she says, "Send me the liquid after disguising the taste, and trust me to do the rest. I must confess I do not understand all you mean by raising the thermometer, Bucha, but you will explain all." This passage shows that Clark had been instructing her how to raise a fictitious temperature, by rubbing the bulb of the thermometer on the bedclothes, or by heating it up in one of the ways favoured by malingerers. He was probably well aware that the atropine and cocaine, which were to be given, could be depended upon to raise Fullam's temperature a few degrees, but this would not be sufficient to produce a really convincing clinical picture of heatstroke. The temperature may rise as high as 107 degrees, or 108 degrees, and certainly will jump up into that neighbourhood, and Clark rightly, from their point of view, insisted on the importance of a thermometer, indicating a very high state of fever, being shown to the doctor who was to be called in. Although Mrs Fullam writes next day, "I will strictly abide by your directions as regards treatment of drenching cold water, &c., also the thermometer," she must have bungled this rather delicate part of the business, as the thermometer never showed more than 100.6 degrees during the whole course of the illness. The absence of a high temperature, such as would be expected in a genuine case of heatstroke, was noted by Major O'Meara, I.M.S., in his evidence at the trial.

The "heatstroke" mixture was duly administered on the night of Thursday, the 27th of July, and on the 28th Mrs Fullam writes:

> They have taken away my dear hubby to the Officers' Ward, in the Station Hospital, after a most dreadful night, more like a nightmare. He is raving with delirium, and quite unconscious. I have just been to see him, 11 a.m., but find no improvement. He has three orderlies looking after him, and they have their work cut out to keep him down.

On the 29th, the details of the administration, and of its results, are related in a long letter:

> To-day he is quite conscious. The fever is only 99, but he is very weak. I am only allowed to stay two or three minutes at his bedside, and he does not say much; he seems quite dazed. I shall tell you, lovie, the whole thing from Thursday night, as I would like you to know all, my own very precious lovie.
>
> I mixed half the dose in his soup that night, but as soon as he tasted it, he sent for the cook and abused him for making such bad soup, so bitter and so full of mustard oil, as he called it, Bucha darling. Anyhow, he had taken about a couple of spoons, and about gun-fire, when we were seated in the garden, Harry darling, he complained of rush of blood to the head, and asked me to pour cold water on his neck and hands, which I did. Then I took his temperature, which was 99.6. So I said, "Eddie, dear, you get into bed and I will give you a dose of fever mixture." So I mixed half of the remaining half into a full dose of diaphoretic,* and took it to him in the dark. He tasted it, and made a very wry face, saying, "Is that fever mixture?" I replied, "Yes! You swallow it quick," and I brought the bottle and the lantern, and he

---

* This was, no doubt, the usual "sweating mixture" familiar in Indian households. It would consist of acetate of ammonium, nitrate of potash, and spirit of nitrous ether.

sat up and read the label, and also smelt the contents, after taking the dose. I then said, "Now go to sleep, and if you want anything you can wake me." My own precious lovie, darling, we both fell asleep, but I not very much, and at 2.30 a.m. he woke me up saying he felt very ill, and was getting paralyzed. I called the ayah, and she and I sat chafing his hands and feet, lovie Bucha. But he asked me to send for Captain Weston, who came and said his heart was failing. Then by 4 a.m. he got worse, my own darling, so I sent the phaeton, and a line to Captain Keene. He came, but my husband was quite delirious. So Captain Keene decided to remove him into hospital at the first flush of daylight, because he said I would never manage him. I told you the three orderlies had their work cut out. He has been very seriously ill, Harry darling, and would have died had the first whole dose gone down. But it was not my fault, Bucha pet, the bitter taste was to blame, and not I, sweetie.

~

July 30th

He is improving slowly but surely… He is very comfortable, and is lying there with the ice bag continually on his head. They have diagnosed the case as heatstroke.

~

July 31st

My hubby is getting on slowly, but surely. The tingling sensations in his feet and hands are just passing off, and he has a normal temperature, only feels weak. The ice bag is still kept constantly on his head, darling, and when I go and see him he talks quite naturally. Another case of heatstroke was taken into the hospital this afternoon, but the man is recovering.

~

> August 9th
>
> Lovie darling, my own precious Harry sweetheart, my hubby was not doing so well when I called to see him last evening. He was not allowed out of bed, and his temperature had gone up to 100.6, the same as it was the night he was taken so bad. So instead of silting outside, as you saw him, Bucha darling, he spent the evening in bed.

By the 14th of August, Fullam, having made a partial recovery, was discharged from hospital, and she writes:

> Everyone thinks they are doing a very foolish thing by sending him home so soon, as the heat is so great and there is fear of a relapse. It is so hard for me, Harry darling, and I only wish it was all over. You should pity and sympathize with me very much, my own darling. He is to continue the hospital mixture of quinine, pill and Mag. sulph. three times a day; also two baths daily and keep very cool.

The "relapse" referred to duly occurred two days afterwards. Though the letters are, for once, silent about the matter—there is a hiatus between August the 14th and the 23rd—the little girl, Kathleen Fullam, gave the following evidence at the trial: "It was in the afternoon when he got ill the second time. He had some medicine. My mother gave it to him. My father was in the dressing-room when my mother gave him the medicine. He drank it, and after drinking it, he said to my mother, after a little while, 'Oh, Gus, you have given me the wrong medicine.' He was taking medicine after coming back from the hospital. When he said that, my mother said that she did not think she had. He said that his throat and tongue were burning. He looked at his tongue in the glass. After that, he ran to his bed. Then he called out for someone to bring him some ice and water. My mother was by his bed, and my brother Frank, who is six, and I were in the drawing-room. There was just a door between. Then he was praying, and saying, 'Oh, God, have mercy on me.'"

Captain Weston, who lived opposite, also testified to having been called in, on this occasion about 4 p.m., and to having found Fullam "unconscious and worse than before". He took him back to hospital immediately. This evidence shows that Mrs Fullam tried the heatstroke once again without success. Fullam again made a bid for recovery, though this second attempt reduced him to a wreck.

> September 2nd
>
> When I called to see my poor hubby this afternoon, I found him not so well. He had passed a restless, wakeful night, with little or no sleep, darling, and the excitement of the P.M.O.'s visit to the hospital this morning was too much for his poor weak nerves. Besides, the Board sits on the case to-day, and so all this put together is worrying him. Oh! I tell you it is a most worrying time for him and me, Harry darling.

During the week following, Fullam improved in health, and again relapsed, and Mrs Fullam is distracted by fear that he may be left on her hands, a chronic invalid. It was one of the strokes of irony of Fate, that she was so often haunted by this fear. There must be few cases known to medical science in which an unfaithful wife, who has made desperate and determined efforts to poison her husband, has been punished by being compelled to nurse a weak, helpless, chronic invalid. It would indeed be a striking instance of the punishment being made to fit the crime. As to this tragic outcome of her crimes, she writes:

September 9th

My husband is very ill. I am the only one allowed to see him. He never speaks to me hardly, but just lies with his eyes closed. He can't walk, as you may suppose, nor can he even sit up, but just twitches, and jumps, and in the intervals stares like a lunatic. What a prospect! But I did it, and so I deserve a ruined life, and a broken home.

Mrs Fullam's letter of the 12th of September contains a dramatic account of an accidental attack of "heatstroke", which occurred to the child Myrtle, as the result of her sucking the bottle:

I did not write the day before yesterday, dear, owing to little Myrtle being ill. I went out on business, my darling, and fancy! She got hold of the bottle containing your famous liquid, which is so deadly certain, and luckily the cork was quite tight, but she sucked all round the cork and when I got home, I snatched it from the little pet, and scolded the ayah for unearthing things I had so carefully put away. Well, Myrtle soon became scarlet, and began to twitch a little, so I kept her in a cold bath and she gradually got much better. But you can fancy my state of mind, Harry darling, and I really thought I would lose her. She must have got very little, thank God!

From this date onwards, until the 7th of October, when he left Agra, Fullam's health improved sufficiently to enable him to be out of hospital. A Medical Board, however, recommended him for eight months' leave, and it is clear from the evidence given at the trial by Major Palmer that he was in a very precarious condition.

In the foregoing account, it has been assumed that the "heatstroke" liquid administered to Fullam owed its poisonous effects to atropine, and cocaine. This was the theory of the Crown, at the trial, and there is much in its favour and little against it. It is, however, more than doubtful whether the prosecution, if it had been obliged to depend upon the medical evidence alone, would have been able to persuade a jury of the guilt of Clark and Mrs Fullam. The letters of the latter made it clear that poison had been administered. The medical evidence, at any rate, was unequivocal as regards arsenic, though not so as regards atropine and cocaine. It was proved in evidence that Clark had purchased atropine on the 23rd, and cocaine on the 26th of July, respectively. The letters showed that he was anxious to produce in the victim unconsciousness, delirium, and high temperature, in order to imitate heatstroke. Atropine and cocaine might be depended upon to do this, and so there was good reason for selecting them. Neither these, nor any other alkaloids, were found in the body of Fullam when it was exhumed, but after such a lapse of time that could not be expected. Against the atropine and cocaine theory, it might have been argued that dilatation of the pupil was not definitely noted as present, and that Fullam had complained of no numbness, or anaesthesia of the mouth and throat, as he might have been expected to do on taking a dose of cocaine. The long delay in the appearance of severe symptoms, after the first "heatstroke" liquid attempt is also curious, but might be explained by the full state of the stomach. An interesting conflict of expert opinion might have been developed round these points, if the central fact of the administration of *some* poison had been less clearly established from the overwhelming testimony of the correspondence.

3

Fullam had arrived in Agra, with his family, on the 8th of October, and he died after dinner on the 10th. The evidence given at the trial by Kathleen, and by the servant, Gir Baksh, leaves little doubt that Fullam was poisoned at dinner, and afterwards, while in bed, by hyperdermic injections given by Clark. These injections probably consisted of the very powerful alkaloid poison, gelsemine, an extract from the root of yellow jasmine, of which a fatal dose is only one-fifth of a grain. The story of this last evening has been told in Section 7 of Chapter II, and it is unnecessary to repeat more than one or two points. During dinner, Fullam became ill, and was helped to his bed, where he vomited. Clark was seen by the child to take a "glass needle", obviously the hyperdermic syringe which was afterwards identified as his—and to fill it with a "white powder" dissolved in water. This he "poked" many times into the body of Fullam. A few minutes after this the child went to her father's bed because she heard him "gargling in his throat". Shortly afterwards, Clark came again to the bedside, felt Fullam's pulse, and, on his return to Mrs Fullam, was heard by the child to say, "Gone!"

Gelsemine was proved to have been purchased by Clark in September, when it could not have been used in Meerut, and forty-eight grains were found in his possession. The page where gelsemine is described in Lyons' "Medical Jurisprudence" was found turned down in Clark's copy. In fact, in both the medico-legal works in Clark's possession, pages were turned down, and underlinings occurred at arsenic, atropine, cocaine and gelsemine. In his confession at the trial, Clark stated that the last injection consisted of digitalis, strychnine and ether, and was intended as a stimulant to the heart, showing that he had done something for the patient, whereas he had given him four drachms of antipyrin "to finish him off". It seems extraordinary that an accused man, with the halter practically round his neck, should go out of his way to make a false statement. Clark, however, seems to have been one of those people who dislike telling the truth if they can possibly lie. The child's clear evidence as to the white powder, dissolved in a wine-glass of water, administered hyperdermically, and followed immediately by death, gives the lie to Clark's confession.

It has already been shown that if the medical evidence had been a serious issue at the trial, it must have been admitted by the Crown that there was none establishing the actual cause of death. Indeed, the Agra Murder case may perhaps be cited to-day as the only one on record, and it will in all likelihood continue to be the only recorded case in the annals of crime, in which a conviction for murder by poisoning was justly recorded without definite proof of the real cause of death. No doubt if Clark had held his tongue, the jury could have been properly directed that they might reasonably infer that a fatal dose of something had been administered to Fullam on the night of his death. The correspondence established that an attempt had been made to get rid of him between April and July by chronic arsenical poisoning, and that further attempts had been made to despatch him by the more summary and decisive method of the "heatstroke" mixture; the fact that he had been reduced to a condition in which his life hung upon a thread, the suspicious nature of his removal to Agra, his sudden attack after eating his dinner, the administration of the hyperdermic injection just before his death, the palpably false death certificate, the trickery adopted by Clark to conceal from Captain Dunne, when he fetched him, that Fullam was already dead, and the method by which he obtained his signature to the death certificate—all these might have been treated by the jury as circumstantial evidence justifying an inference of guilt. But this chain of reasoning became superfluous, and the medical cause of death became irrelevant, from the moment that Clark made his statement from the dock. He was not bound to make it, but the law did not allow him to give evidence. The Court was bound to put questions to him, asking him if he wished to explain anything in the evidence which appeared to be against him. He lied in detail, but told the truth in substance, with an impudent assumption of humane compassion, when he explained that he saw that Fullam was doomed, and gave the antipyrin "to finish him off". Probably Clark's last falsehood from the dock was told with a view to carrying out the design which he had formed, and which he pursued throughout the trial, of accepting full responsibility for the final act which took Fullam's life, and of exculpating his mistress. Because the fact is, and it was fully established by the evidence of Kathleen, and Gir Baksh, that Fullam's last dinner, which must have contained some form of poison, probably arsenic, was given to Fullam by the hand of his wife alone.

The medical evidence given at the trial, though it confirms the history of Fullam's frequent attacks, and long illness in Meerut, does not contribute much to the scientific analysis of the case. The post-mortem examination, conducted by Major O'Meara, I.M.S., Civil Surgeon of Agra, on the 6th of December, 1912, one year, one month, and twenty-six days after death, and the subsequent analysis by the Chemical Examiner, disclosed no alkaloids, and no ptomaines. The viscera were in an advanced state of decomposition. The extract, which was obtained by the Stas-Otto method, was tested for strychnine, gelsemine, digitalin, atropine, and cocaine, with negative results. No arsenic was found in the hair, or in the earth inside the coffin, but arsenic was found in the bones. The half of the thigh bone contained about .015 grains of arsenic. The body was in a peculiar state of decomposition. The muscles were very well preserved, and of a dark red colour. The diaphragm and the intestines were extremely well preserved, and so were the heart and liver. As will appear, the Civil Surgeon was of opinion that these appearances indicated chronic administration of arsenic.

The death certificate stated that E.M. Fullam had been suffering from "general paralysis", for the past three months, and having had a relapse, had died from heart failure at 9.30 p.m. on the 10th of October, 1911. This document was, of course, a tissue of lies. A pencil draft of it, in Clark's handwriting, was found in the despatch box, in which the correspondence was discovered. The original was signed by Captain Dunne, R.A.M.C. Clark's official status did not entitle him to give a death certificate, without a counter-signature by a superior officer. As Fullam was in the Military Accounts Department, and had been in a military hospital, Captain Dunne's signature was considered sufficient. The reader has already seen, in Section 7 of Chapter II, the circumstances under which Captain Dunne was induced to sign the certificate. He was brought over from England to give evidence at the trial. He stated that he knew Clark, and had confidence in him. It may here be observed that, if he had any confidence in either Clark's capacity or character, his knowledge of him must have been of the slightest. He added that as Clark had had charge of the invalid, which really was not the case, he accepted his statements. But he had not seen the deceased while he was alive, and Captain Dunne was rebuked by the Chief Justice at the trial, for having signed a certificate containing statements of which he had no personal knowledge. Without this counter-signature, it is probable that there would have been a difficulty about the burial, and it is certain that the least check of this kind would have led to the immediate discovery of the crime. It may be said that during all this critical time, Clark, aided by his courage and cunning, experienced considerable good fortune.

After proof had been given of the poison purchased by Clark, Captain Weston, retired I.S.M.D., "that old duffer opposite", to quote Mrs Fullam, though she was quite wrong, was the first medical witness called at the trial. He related the incidents of the poisoning by arsenic in June, and of the two "heatstroke" attacks in July and August, with which the reader is already familiar. He alone appears to have suspected arsenic, and to have warned Fullam on the subject. He had, however, thought that the two subsequent attacks were genuine cases of heatstroke, and he said positively that Fullam had no history of paralysis, although he had been given to understand by Mrs Fullam, when her husband got leave from the Medical Board, that it was on the ground of "general paralysis of the insane". He seems to have known nothing at all about the symptoms of poisoning by cocaine, or atropine, and to have been a gentleman whose suspicions were not easily aroused.

Major Palmer, R.A.M.C., who was in charge of the Military Hospital at Meerut in July 1911, was the next witness. He did not remember much about Fullam's case, except what he was able to glean by refreshing his memory from the casebook. He regarded the case, at the first visit in July, as one of heatstroke, although the temperature did not rise above 101, which all the doctors agreed was exceptionally low for heatstroke, in which it rises as high as 106, or 107. He remembered that the patient suffered from extreme muscular weakness, and that he was emotional, with the mind of a child; easily influenced, and easily moved to tears. On the occasion of the return to hospital in August, the second case of supposed heatstroke, there was the same muscular weakness, which Major Palmer described as "paresis" rather than paralysis, and which puzzled him a good deal at the time. It was an unusual mode of the advent of paralysis, which was dismissed as out of the question. But its peculiar persistence, and the patient's incapacity for any mental effort, such as signing an assignment of his pay to his wife, were regarded as unusual concomitants of heatstroke. Major Palmer added that the persistent muscular weakness, and the mental condition which he had noticed, might have been the results of chronic arsenical poisoning, though that had not suggested itself to anyone at the time, to his knowledge. He also said that he would have expected more dilatation of the pupil if the patient had been given atropine or cocaine. Major Palmer had signed the certificate recommending Fullam, on the 13th of August, 1911, for leave of absence in England, stating that eight months' treatment and rest were absolutely necessary for his recovery. He allowed the discharge from hospital on the 14th of August, but recognized the possibility of a relapse. 1911 was one of the hottest years within living memory in India, and the rains did not break in Meerut until September, which meant an exceptionally trying and difficult time for everybody. There were several cases in hospital of heatstroke, and four or five deaths from it. Major Palmer was generally of opinion that, if the original complaint had been really due to heatstroke, Fullam might easily have had another which would have killed him, though not so late in the year at Agra as the second week in October. But if the original attacks were due to poison, he would have eventually recovered, if he had not been given a fresh dose.

Major O'Meara, the Civil Surgeon of Agra who conducted the post-mortem upon Fullam's corpse, was the last medical witness, but was certainly also the most illuminating. He said that he had no expectation of finding alkaloids in the body after the expiration of fourteen months in the Plains, but that he sent the thigh bone, as containing the greatest amount of compact tissue, to be tested for arsenic, because of the remarkable state of preservation of several parts of the corpse. It is a disputed point whether arsenic preserves, but the balance of evidence is that it does, and the condition of the muscles struck Major O'Meara very forcibly as resembling the condition which he had seen in the dissecting room, where arsenic had been used as a preservative. Major O'Meara added that, in his opinion, the paresis which had been spoken of by Major Palmer, or, in other words, peripheral neuritis, or inflammation of the nerves of the extremities, was a symptom of chronic arsenical poisoning, and not of atropine or cocaine, and also that the temperature which Fullam had was not high enough to be the probable result of natural heatstroke. It was this witness who found the pages turned down in Clark's book, and he was the one witness who, at the conclusion of his evidence, definitely enunciated the opinion that Fullam had been eventually despatched by a hyperdermic injection of gelsemine, hydrochloride, or of some strong alkaloid, which in Fullam's then condition, would have been enough to kill him, and which would have been difficult, if not impossible, to discover in the corpse, fourteen months after death.

IV

The Two Trials

As already observed, the trials for the two Agra murders possess little interest either of a forensic, or of a legal character. There were certain peculiar features about the procedure, which on that account are deserving of passing notice. But except for the morbid excitement usually associated with a sensational *crime passionel*, and for the curiosity aroused amongst the public by the appearance in the dock of the two chief culprits, there was no great interest in the forensic display. But as long as Mrs Fullam and Clark remained in the dock, the Sessions Court of the Allahabad High Court was crowded with a body of spectators such as has never been seen there before or since, and special arrangements had to be made by the police for the accommodation of those who were drawn there by the exceptional nature of the case.

The trial of Mrs Fullam and Clark for the murder of Mr Fullam was held first on the 27th of February, 1913, and occupied three days. Nearly a day and a half of this was taken up by the opening for the Crown,* which necessarily consisted of the reading of long and numerous extracts from the correspondence with which the reader is already familiar. The accused had been committed, and were arraigned, on two charges. First, with having attempted to murder Mr Fullam between the months of April and October, 1911, and secondly, with his murder on the 10th of October. The Crown were obviously well advised in framing the charges in this way, apart from the fact that the linking of alternative, or cumulative, charges is a familiar feature of criminal trials in India, because, as we have already seen in the preceding chapter, there was no clear medical evidence to establish the actual cause of the death of Mr Fullam on the fatal evening.

On the other hand, the compromising nature of the long correspondence, the statement which Mrs Fullam had already made before the Magistrate admitting the crime, and seeking to exculpate herself by claiming to have been hypnotized by Clark, and to have acted throughout under his influence, and the letter which she had sent from jail, and which appears in facsimile in this book, rendered a good deal of what one may call the historical evidence, which had been tendered before the Magistrate, altogether superfluous.

Mr Sarkies, who was employed in the Military Accounts Department at Meerut, under Fullam, gave the story of his

* The following counsel appeared: For the Crown, Mr A.E. Ryves, Government Advocate (afterwards Mr Justice Ryves), Mr M. Malcolmson, Assistant Government Advocate, and Mr (now Sir) C. Boss Alston. For Clark, Mr E.A. Howard, barrister, and Mr O.M. Chiene, vakil; for Mrs Fullam, Mr R.K. Sorabji and Mr A.H.M. Hamilton, barristers; for the Indian accused, Mr Ishaq Khan and Mr Ahmed Karim, vakils.

home life, his general state of health, and his attacks of illness in the hot weather of 1911. He entirely negatived the theory that Fullam had ever shown signs of general paralysis. Nothing was said at the trial about the talk which had taken place in the circle in which the Fullams lived in Meerut about the relations between Mrs Fullam and Clark, nor of the ugly rumours which had obtained vogue when Fullam's death at Agra became known. Plenty of evidence of this kind was available, and it is one of the mysterious features of the case that it never occurred to any one in Meerut to mention it to the police at the time of Fullam's death. The Meerut postmaster gave evidence of Mrs Fullam having received in the false name of "Mrs Clarkson" a continuous succession of letters and parcels from Agra. Evidence was given by a number of chemists of the supply to Clark of a large quantity of arsenic, and various alkaloids, which it was clear had been administered to Fullam. The medical evidence, which has been summarized in the preceding chapter, was called, and finally little Kathleen Fullam, an exceptionally intelligent child of ten, told the pathetic story of her father's death, which appears in Section 7 of Chapter II. This concluded the evidence for the Crown, and, in answer to the Court, Clark then made the following statement from the dock:

> I wish to say that I am wholly and solely to blame. Mrs Fullam was acting under my direction. I, having the stronger will, had her under my control. Whatever drugs were given, I sent. She acted under my influence. She is not to blame for what she did, I am to blame for the whole thing.
>
> May I speak from the beginning, your Lordship? At the beginning I had the intention only of making him sick, and

by giving him small doses of poison just enough to make him ill, to get him sent away on long leave out of the country.

The correspondence clearly shows that this, again, was a falsehood, and that determined efforts had been made to kill the unfortunate man outright. Mrs Fullam apologizes, in one letter, for not having given enough of the "heatstroke" mixture, when Fullam had nearly died, and says that it was not her fault. Indeed, to have got Fullam out of the country on leave would have put an end to her matrimonial scheme, which the letters show was what she valued most. Clark continued:

> The effects of the last doses he got in July and August made him very ill, and he came to Agra in a dying condition. When he came to Agra I was very sorry for the condition I saw him in, because he was physically a wreck. I simply administered four drahms of antipyrin before dinner to kill him. I gave him the antipyrin when he was physically a wreck, to finish him, and it was that which killed him. It was not the injections. The injections consisted of digitalis, strychnine and ether, but the doses were too small to counteract the effects of the antipyrin which was given before dinner. The latter is what played upon his heart. I gave but two injections, one under the heart, and one in the arm. They were only given to show that I was trying to do something for him when he was in that weak condition. I knew they would do no good.

Reasons have already been given in the preceding chapter for thinking that this statement also was untrue. It is significant that Clark said nothing to Captain Dunne, when he called him in after Fullam's death, about the injections which he had given him to try and do him good.

Mrs Fullam's statement is not worth reproducing. She merely pretended that she wanted to make her husband ill, and not to kill him, and that she gave half, and quarter, doses of what Clark sent her, because she thought that full doses would be fatal. She was a woman who could persuade herself of anything. She had obviously been advised to write the letter which appears in this book. She could have had little hope of escape after the petition in that letter had been ignored, and that door was closed. She had nothing to fear from a sentence of death. She knew she would not be hanged, as she was pregnant, and in the condition known to English law as "quick with child". She wrote her letter from prison, just a fortnight before her trial:

To The Joint Magistrate

Dear Sir,

I have been considering over my case, and feel perfectly distracted and worried in mind, so much so that I feel it is my duty in the sight of God, and for the sake of all justice and truth, to turn "King's Evidence" on both cases.

May I beg you, therefore, kindly to forward this my appeal to the Honble. High Court, Allahabad for due consideration.

I remain,

Dear Sir,

Yours faithfully,

A. Fullam

It was a desperate throw for safety. She was far too intelligent to suppose that her evidence was required for the sake of truth.

After Clark's confession the trial was, to all intents and purposes, at an end. Clark's counsel did not address the jury, while Mrs Fullam's contented himself with asking them to accept the view that she was under Clark's influence, and did not seek her husband's death. The summing-up was short, and dealt mainly with this last issue. The jury, after considering for about two minutes, naturally convicted both the accused. Evidence was then given by the Assistant Civil Surgeon as to Mrs Fullam's condition, and for some reason which does not appear, sentences were postponed.

The trial of the second case was also postponed, for some reason or other, until the following Monday week, and took place on the 10th, 11th, 12th and 13th of March. There were six accused. The charge was that of having murdered Mrs Clark, the wife of Lieut. Clark, one of the accused, at her bungalow, on the night of the 17th of November, 1912. The four principal accused were India bazaar badmashes, or loafing ruffians. Buddha, kanjar, aged 23; Ram Lal, kachi, aged 22; Sukkha, darzi, aged 20; and Mohan, bharbhuja, aged 20. They were mere hired assassins. Mrs Fullam, and Clark, were charged with them for having abetted the commission of the crime. The correspondence was quite enough to convict them, and the child, Kathleen Fullam, had overheard her mother and Clark giving instructions to some of the accused. Mrs Fullam and Clark pleaded guilty to this offence. They were thereupon sentenced to death, both for the murder of Fullam, and also for the murder of Mrs Clark to which they had just pleaded guilty. Mrs Fullam's sentence was then, in accordance with the statutory provision, commuted to one of transportation for life. For some reason the Chief

Justice sentenced her to "penal servitude" in both cases, although this is a sentence unknown to Indian law. The two convicts were then removed, and all public interest in the proceedings came to an end. Miss Clark and Kathleen Fullam gave evidence, but the main testimony against the accused consisted of the evidence of the approver, Buddhu, the unmitigated scoundrel, whose character has been already described in Section 8 of Chapter II. He had confessed to the midnight murder of Mrs Clark, no doubt with a view to being called as a witness and pardoned. He was just the type of scamp who frequently succeeds, in India, in escaping the just punishment for his misdeeds, and with whom all those who have any experience of crime in India are so familiar. The difficulty of procuring independent and truthful evidence is notorious. But Indian criminals usually commit their crimes in gangs. Apart from their lack of physical courage, they seem to think that if a sufficient number of their relations and friends are associated with them, there will be less chance of their being "given away". The truth is precisely the converse. When clues begin to be found, and the scent begins to grow strong, fear and self-preservation become the dominant motives of the accused, and there is usually a race, generally won by the most experienced in criminality, to get to the police, and to "blow the gaff". It is probably true to say that a large proportion of criminals in Indian jails have been sent there by their relations and friends.

Buddhu, the approver in this case, did his work well, and obtained his pardon. As he was probably the ringleader under Clark, he knew all about it, and all the Crown had to do was to obtain corroboration of his evidence. This was forthcoming from Kathleen, and certain Indian witnesses upon whose evidence it is unnecessary to dwell. The accused called no evidence, and each adopted the familiar defence of telling a long and complicated story of their absence from the scene of the crime, and of their occupation at the time in other pursuits. Ram Lal succeeded in securing a majority of the jury in his favour. A certain proportion not unusually do. Ram Lal must be considered to have been fortunate. The verdict of the majority in his favour was accepted, probably because it was not worthwhile to try him all over again, when five of the murderers were condemned to death. There was no special reason why the informer should have falsely named him, and the latter was treated as having kept his part of the bargain by telling the truth. Buddha, Sukkha and Mohan were sentenced to death. It is a peculiarity of their trial, which can very rarely have occurred, that they were tried in the High Court by a European jury. In the ordinary way they would have been tried at Sessions, by the Sessions Judge, without a jury, though with assessors. But Mrs Fullam and Clark were entitled to trial in the High Court, and to a jury, and the four Indian accused were charged with them. In consequence of their plea of "Guilty", the two former were not tried at all, so the latter had a High Court Judge and jury all to themselves. Ram Lal almost certainly owed his escape to this circumstance. General satisfaction was expressed that justice had at last been done, especially amongst those in Meerut who had always believed that Fullam had been foully done to death, and the police were congratulated upon the skill and celerity with which they acted in securing the conviction of the perpetrators of these two exceptional crimes.

Allahabad.
12th February 1913.

To the Jews - Hospital.

Dear Sir,

I have been enumerating over my case & feel perfectly distracted & worried in mind so much so that I feel it — is my duty in the sight of God & for the sake of all justice & truth, to turn "King's Evidence" in both cases.

I beg I say you therefore kindly to forward this my appeal to the Honble High Court,

Allahabad for their consideration —

I remain
dear Sir
Yours faithfully
A. Fullam

V

OBITER DICTA

One notable feature about this double drama was its reception by the public in India. It was a "nine days' wonder", and when the trials were over it was forgotten. Both the trials were dull, although the personalities of the two chief culprits excited a certain morbid curiosity. None of the lawyers engaged were able to lift them above the commonplace, and the result was always a foregone conclusion. A search for contemporaneous criticism discloses little more than astonishment and disgust that such things should be, and satisfaction that the English police officers had brought the murderers to justice. No one appears to have been struck by the psychological aspects of the case. And yet there are few stories of guilty passion, either in history or in fiction, which present more puzzling features. For though the plans which Clark and Mrs Fullam made between April 1911, and November 1912, for murdering their respective spouses, were cold-blooded enough, and were carried through with wonderful persistence and determination, yet they were merely the outcome of a passion which seems to have possessed no motive force but the springs of an ungovernable lust. Divorce was surely simpler and quicker and not more shameful than murder. The position of Mrs Fullam and Clark was such that though their passion burned with unquenchable fire, it had no material advantages, and no real happiness, to offer to either of them, but only certain embarrassment even if they could have been married.

What was there about Clark which enabled him to acquire such sway over women in general, and over Mrs Fullam in particular? She was not lacking, as her letters show, in refinement, sweetness of disposition and true womanliness. She had a happy home, and intelligent children. But Clark, although clever and cunning where his own interests were concerned, had no intellectual gifts. His appearance, as we have seen, was almost repulsive. He looked like a stupid man, and a sensualist. He was dirty, both in appearance and in his habits. Nonetheless, he was successful with women. It was believed, as we have already seen, that he was of special service to some who had need of unprofessional treatment, from a professional man, and if there is any truth in this, the mutual regard which was said to exist between him and the lady members of the society in which he moved, may have received an incentive which had nothing to do with personal attractiveness. Yet he undoubtedly had many amours. Mrs Fullam's outbreaks of jealousy were not without reason. But even she, who demanded all in all from him, was prepared, if one may judge from her flippant reference to "black hens", to regard with toleration the visits which he was known to make, from time to time, to women in the bazaar.

It is surprising, though not unprecedented, that a man built in so coarse a mould should have succeeded with two women so unlike each other as his own wife and Mrs Fullam. But though a woman never mistakes a good man for a bad man, she will often mistake a bad man for a good one. Probably Mrs Clark had never given him her heart. She had none of the fascination and natural intelligence which enable a wife to influence and control a wild and masterful man such as her brutish husband unquestionably was. She possessed a strong sense of duty, and that sort of meekness and docility which, if they do not happen to attract, are certain in the end rather to repel, and to aggravate the temper which they are intended to soothe. The caustic letter written by the daughter to her father, in defence of her mother, throws light upon Clark's early courtship, though at the same time one feels a certain scepticism about the taunt that Mrs Clark had refused many better offers. The explanation of Mrs Clark's conduct is that her marriage was one of *convenance*, and that having made the mistake of her life, she had sufficient patience and power of endurance to make the best of it. She devoted herself to her children and they were devoted to her, repaying her mother's love with interest. Their demeanour, when they had to give evidence against their father, did them credit, though it showed how far, by his conduct towards them, he had drifted from their affection and regard. Mrs Clark knew quite well that he would have poisoned her if she had not been so wide-awake. She had the safeguard of those who are so constituted as to vomit on the least provocation, and to this unpleasant quality she probably owed several years of life. "Why is Mr Clark so angry with me and my children?" she pleadingly asks in her written soliloquy. The answer is obvious. They cost him money for their support, and they interfered with the full enjoyment of his selfish propensities. But she, worthy soul, turns aside the greater condemnation, and finds an excuse for her "lord and master", in the bad company he had got into since he came to Agra.

Mrs Fullam presents an almost insoluble problem. Of the depth of her affection for Clark, of its abandonment of self, and, up to a point, of its fidelity, there is no question. This aspect of her conduct presents no difficulties. Her happiness, after her husband is out of the way, and she can enjoy Clark's society, almost when she likes, is complete. She was of a naturally warm nature, which she had succeeded in subduing, until she met her fate. She was undoubtedly religious, and for many years she was a good wife, and a fond mother. Hers is a typical case of what the French call "La Grande Passion". Unfortunately for her, Clark was her passion, and her ruin. But what she saw in "that awful feller", as his contemporaries called him, none of her friends in Meerut could ever understand. The explanation probably is that she found in him that virility, and strength of passion, which drew out, and fed, the latent fires of her own nature.

She may have inherited this capacity for an ungovernable passion. She was superior, probably in birth, certainly in education and intellect, to the other three actors in this drama. She had been a pretty young girl, bright and buxom, though after her marriage she became distinctly stout, a habit of body against which she utters only a feeble protest. She appreciated admiration, and enjoyed going out and "having a good time", but she was not thought to be a flirt, and it was said of her that "she would have smacked the face of any young man who attempted to take a liberty with her." Her leanings towards religion did not leave her even in her most abandoned moments. She had taught in the Sunday School as a girl, and she deliberately chose Fullam, who was a quiet man and an earnest Sunday School teacher. In a worldly sense, she had done very well. This makes her surrender to Clark all the more difficult to understand. Fullam's income was double that of Clark, and, as invariably occurs in this rank of life in India, his superiority in every worldly respect, was on the same scale.

Until Mrs Fullam met Clark, she had had a quiet and happy home. She may at times have found it dull. It would not be a large assumption. Her husband was a retiring man, and would have been well suited with Mrs Clark as his wife, in spite of the inferiority of her intellect and education. Such is life! Mrs Fullam's letters, though they contain excessive sentimentality and "gush", in the cheap novelette style, mixed with vulgar poetry, and occasional grammatical lapses, indicate strength of character, a keen sense of humour, and considerable power of expression. The truth is that she possessed one of those natures, partly spiritual, but chiefly animal, which, in affairs of the heart, like "to be taken by storm". She was subconsciously a victim of Sadism. She lived in a world of romance, and gloried in erotic topics, and sexual gossip, but she would not tolerate bestiality in cold-blood. She discloses this part of her inner nature by the letter in which she asks Clark not to send her, and advises him not to read, gross literature. Yet some of her letters are unfit for publication. She loved to be petted, but she wanted to be smacked. She sought admiration, but she wanted domination. Her vision of Clark leading her to the Hymeneal Altar, "under arched swords of your brother officers, darling," her anxiety when Clark lost his gold family crest, and her pride in her "Pedigree Gentleman", though it is problematical whether his ancient lineage was anything to be proud of, are sidelights on this phase of her character. She would not have raised much objection, we may surmise, if she had happened to be one of the Sabine woman. In the early days of the intrigue, when her infatuation for Clark was passing into the stage of a burning passion, she writes and tries to rebuke him, both for his treatment of his own wife, and for his marked attentions to herself. She promises to talk him into "sound sense and proper reasoning", but she must needs go on to add that, when he is with her she becomes utterly weak, and is like wax in his hands. Could she have written anything more utterly foolish? George Eliot somewhere says that women would be spared half their sufferings if they would only refrain from saying what they are prompted to utter, when they know before they utter it that it would be better left unsaid. From the moment when Mrs Fullam wrote in this way to a man like Clark, her doom was sealed.

Throughout the long and passionate correspondence she presents constant problems. She is an exasperating example of the baffling inconsistencies of the "eternal feminine". Her final attempt at self-condonation by her assertion that she was not a free agent because she was hypnotized by Clark, may be dismissed as a foolish, though intelligible, effort to find a way of escape from the toils which were closing on her. But the illustration which she gave in her confession before the Magistrate of an occasion when Clark, by the mere power of his glance, compelled her husband to go to his office, and stay there all day, when he felt unwell and did not want to go, cannot be mere invention, and her account of it carries conviction.

Mrs Fullam was disillusioned about Clark before the end. It is possible that she tried to persuade him against the second murder, though she did not possess the moral courage to warn Mrs Clark. It is possible that she would have preferred to remain as Clark's mistress in her own apartments with her children, and with his support, to the risk of entering into the matrimonial bond from which there would be no escape. There was certainly nothing mercenary in her betrayal of her husband and her surrender to Clark's advances. But here, if the supposition is correct, she did Clark less than justice. He no doubt found life intolerable with his own wife, though it was no fault of the wife's. He might well have murdered her even though there were no Mrs Fullam. But he had already run enormous risks and made considerable sacrifices for his mistress. To the end he showed no sign of cooling down and deserting her. When the Medical Board, during Mr Fullam's illness, suggested that he should retire to England, which meant final separation for all time from Clark, Mrs Fullam, for a moment, rounded on Clark, and complained that he had not completed the kill with one big dose. His subsequent conduct must have convinced her that the charge of supineness was an unjust one, and that he was prepared to do his best, which he certainly did. When she finally complained before the Magistrate that Clark had deceived her, and asked God to forgive him, as she had forgiven, she was expecting to bear him a child. So that either something had occurred between them during the last few weeks of their intimacy in Agra to convince her that he was unworthy of her supreme devotion, or she presents a problem of irreconcilable motives, which cannot be solved by the mere suggestion that at the last moment she decided to appeal to those considerations of sex, which often save a woman from the gallows, and sometimes from an adequate punishment for her sin. Her explanation that intervention to prevent the murder of Mrs Clark would only have postponed it, is merely another instance of her weakness and lack of moral courage. She even comforted herself with the belief in her Maker, and in the dispensations of an all-guiding Providence, while her hands were steeped in blood. When the end came she resigned herself to her fate, not so much with stoicism, as with penitence, and when she received the sentence of death, although she had had nine days to prepare herself for the ordeal, she sank back into her chair and sobbed aloud.

The criminal intrigue between Lieutenant Clark and Mrs Fullam, ending in the cold-blooded poisoning of the woman's husband after many futile attempts, has been likened to the Thompson-Bywaters case, which occurred at Ilford in the winter of 1922. Yet there is, in truth, little resemblance between the two crimes. Both women had good husbands, and no temptation to get rid of them if they had not fallen victims to an overmastering passion. But Mrs Thompson was older, more experienced, and of stronger mould than her lover, whom she had known well from a boy. Hers was the mastermind which conceived the course of crime upon which the two embarked, and planned the various steps which they undertook. Bywaters worshipped her, and believed in her. She was the temptress, and by far the more determined sinner of the two. And she crowned her villainy with unspeakable treachery and cowardice. Young Bywaters was the one who was deluded, and his discovery of the woman's real character completed the sorrow of his unhappy fate, and in all likelihood reconciled him to the gallows. But Mrs Fullam fell a victim to the wiles and gallantry of Clark, and surrendered herself to his will to such an extent that, although she was happy with her husband and her children, and occasionally reminded Clark of his duty to his wife, she seemed powerless to resist his murderous schemes. She faltered, but stuck loyally to him, and although in an effort to do justice to herself, she blamed the stronger will which had dominated her, she told the truth throughout, and did not attempt to conceal her complicity. It would have been idle to have done otherwise, but though it was equally idle on the part of Mrs Thompson, she went into the witness-box and invented a mendacious story designed to throw the whole of the responsibility for the crime on to her lover, and to save herself. Though both women showed courage, particularly in the execution of the final plan, Mrs Thompson betrayed a meanness when all was over, from which Mrs Fullam was wholly free. The boldness of the Clark-Fullam conspiracy, amounting as it did to effrontery, in its closing stages and the second desperate throw, is extraordinary. After having, by a combination of courage and good fortune, achieved their main object, successfully covered up their tracks, and buried the past, getting into port, so to speak, after a stormy voyage, and after running enormous risks, how was it that they tempted fortune again by the desperate and horrible murder of Mrs Clark? This is a matter which affects the character of Clark rather than that of Mrs Fullam. And in this connection the case of this abandoned scoundrel bears a certain resemblance to that of the Hay solicitor, Armstrong, who was hung in 1922, for the murder of his wife, effected by administering arsenic. He had done it with success, though it seemed afterwards that he had had little to gain from it. He had covered up his tracks and buried the past. Yet a year later, just at a year after the death of Mr Fullam, Clark finally resolved to kill his own wife, Armstrong started a scheme of poisoning a brother solicitor for an utterly paltry motive. It is likely that in each case the appetite for another attempt had been excited by the success of the first venture in crime, and that a desperate courage, fomented by a sort of vanity, urged each to try his luck again. No other explanation is really adequate. And in the case of both Armstrong and Clark, a mysterious fatalism led to the discovery of their crimes. The former actually kept compromising packets of arsenic in the drawer of his writing table, and carried one about in his pocket, Clark's conduct is still more difficult to understand. In Mrs Fullam's room, where he spent most of his spare time after she became a widow and came to live in Agra, and where, if suspicion pointed to him, a search was certain to be made, he kept the despatch box, practically unguarded, containing something like 400 useless love letters, carefully tied in bundles, and endorsed in his handwriting, almost any one of which, if it fell into the hands of a public-spirited citizen, to say nothing of an official or a member of the police force, was enough to send him to the gallows for the murder of his friend Fullam. Why did he keep them? He was far from being a mere love-sick sentimentalist.

He was a coarse, selfish brute, versed in the art of planning and concealing villainy. The method by which he obtained the certificate of death in the case of Mr Fullam was masterly. It is well-nigh impossible to suggest a reasonable explanation of this last piece of folly, unless one is to attribute it to that species of fatalism which plays so large a part in the philosophy of Indian life. One can only say that by one of the mysterious dispensations of Providence, he chose to do it, and thereby, like many another otherwise successful criminal, put the rope round his own neck. If he had destroyed the letters—and it is strange indeed, that Mrs Fullam did not see that he did—he probably would have escaped the penalty of his crimes, and would certainly have removed the exceptional material now available for preserving a record of this grim tragedy.

From the moment of the seizure of the despatch box by the police, both of them must have known that the game was up. Whatever motive Clark had for preserving the letters, he was cunning enough to leave them in Mrs Fullam's custody. They both lived with only a tin box between them and the gallows, in the same kind of security which people accept who reside under the lee of a dormant, but occasionally active, volcano. When Inspector Smith accidentally kicked his foot against the box—by such slender threads do our lives hang—Mrs Fullam turned crimson, and "sank in a heap on a chair". Neither of the accused showed the slightest disposition to fight from the moment they were charged. This is unusual in India, no matter how desperate the case. Clark, a gambler to the core, took little apparent interest in the legal proceedings, with the exception of a question or two on some medical point. When he made his last statement, at his trial in the High Court, he did his best to save Mrs Fullam, but he lied once more. He made a feeble sort of bid for public sympathy by pretending that the final act by which he took Fullam's life, was an act of mercy to put him out of his misery. But on the whole he showed merely a morose and dogged indifference, and he received his sentence and went to his execution with the same appearance of unconcern. He was certainly not lacking in courage, with a large endowment of "the fatalism of the East", and it is impossible to deny his possession of qualities which usually make for success in life, if only they are accompanied by character. He was faithful to the end to the woman who had sacrificed herself for him; at least, as faithful as he could ever be to anyone; and his last request in jail, before his death, was to be allowed to see her. This, according to the rules, would have been granted, but Mrs Fullam refused to meet him.

We have seen how, for two years, this strange woman lived a life of duplicity and crime, and yet never lost touch with the religious notions in which she had been brought up, and which coloured much of her daily thought and life at home. All through this tragic phase, she was constantly conscience-smitten, and she passed her fourteen months of prison life, in full repentance, according to her lights. She was under the charge of Colonel Hudson, I.M.S., the Governor of Naini Jail, one of the ablest and most humane men in that great medical service. He often said that he believed in her contrition, and that he could not understand how a woman of such sweet and attractive nature, and of apparently tender conscience, could have been guilty of such conduct. Her behaviour in prison was exemplary. I had the advantage of hearing about her life there, from a nurse employed in the jail infirmary, who helped her through her confinement in July 1913, and nursed her during her last illness in May 1914. But though she suffered the pangs of remorse and underwent much physical torture from the terrific heat, during the two hot weathers she passed in prison, she retained, in large measure, her natural gaiety. She would sing and joke, and laugh with the other female prisoners and with the Indian wardresses, who regarded her as a "narty"—their word for flightiness. Anything like high spirits is looked upon, amongst Indian women, as an indication of loose character. She impressed upon all of them never to trust a man. What grievances she had against the only two in whom she had put her trust, it would be difficult to say. But she had persuaded herself that Clark was wholly to blame for her fall, though she recognized the justice of her punishment. It was "poetic justice", if ever there were such a thing, that she should have died of "heatstroke". No punkahs, but only portable hand fans, were supplied to prisoners in those days. She had been accustomed to obtain relief from the intense heat by going to the Hills, and she was not of a build to be able to withstand for long the strain of the blazing heat of a prison in the Plains. She nursed her baby (which was afterwards adopted by some kind people) bravely and well, but the time came when she longed for death, and the end must have come as a merciful release.

www.ingramcontent.com/pod-product-compliance
Lightning Source LLC
Chambersburg PA
CBHW052051220426
3663CB00012B/2530